AF477856

Louise Fishman

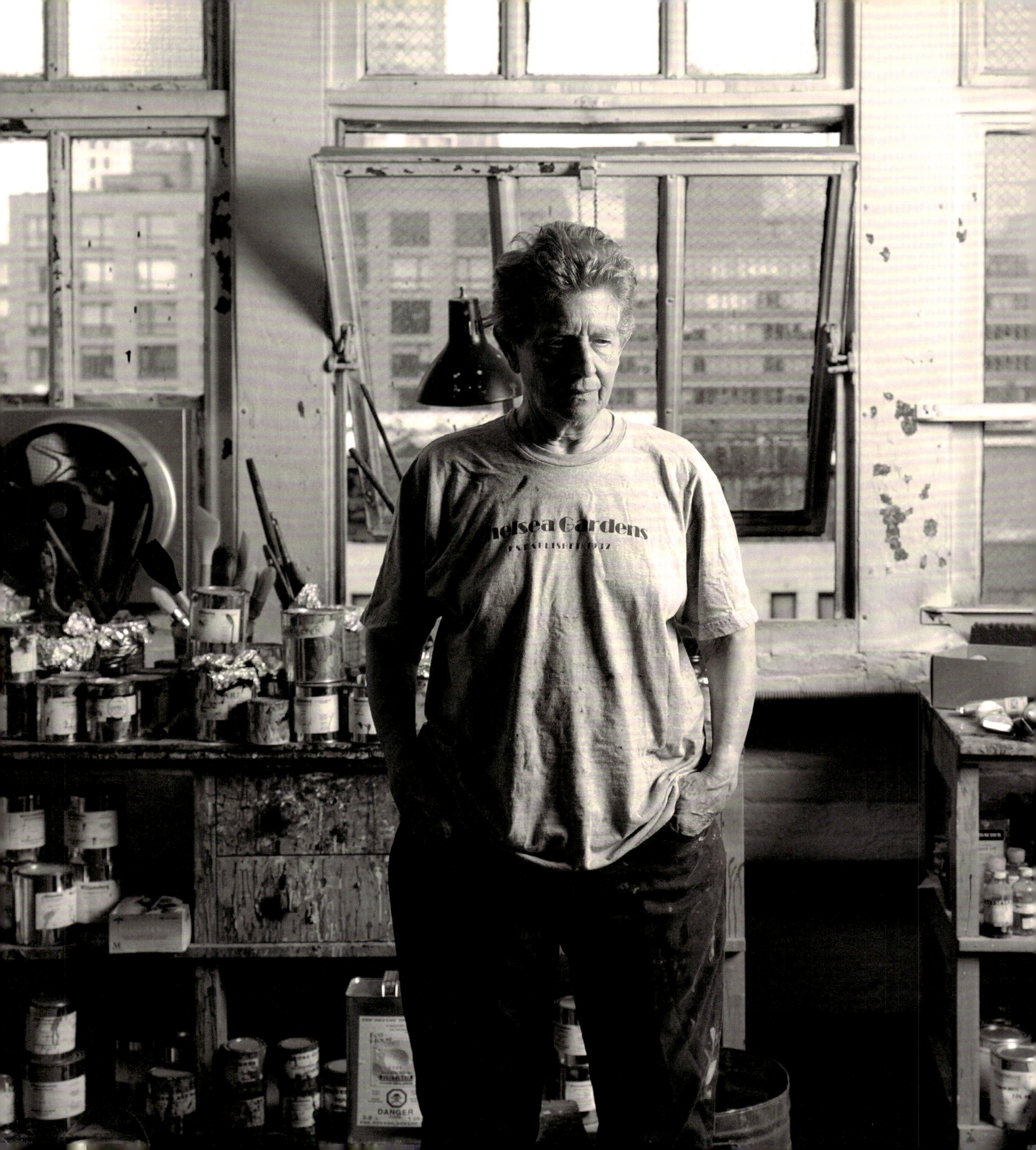
helsea Gardens
DANGER

Louise Fishman

Cheim & Read
2017

Doing and Undoing: On Some Recent Paintings by Louise Fishman

Aruna D'Souza

Louise Fishman's *A Little Ramble* (plate 25) is oceanic and atmospheric, aqueous and gaseous, watery and airy at once.

At first read, you might think I'm saying this because the painting is overwhelmingly, luxuriously blue, the color of sea and sky and many things besides—but that's not it. Yes, there are blues—ranging from pale, transparent blue-green to deep teal to ultramarine to blue-black—but there are also forest and drab greens, whites, umbers, and even, if my eyes don't deceive me, bits of red.

Each of these pigments has a distinctly different coloristic and optical effect depending on how it is applied—whether troweled on thick as plaster by a wide knife, dragged by a scraper across the nubby canvas, diluted and painted in thin washes, squeezed directly from the tube, pressed on using a bit of paper, cardboard and strips of painter's tape, at times left in place, at others peeled off, leaving an irregular, raised pattern behind (the Surrealists called this technique "decalcomania"), or laid on in one of the myriad other ways that Fishman manages to get paint on canvas. The surface is the site of an endlessly fascinating array of light effects as a result, ranging from transparency to opacity, from matteness to opalescence.

This play of color, brushstroke, and luminosity—and there is, in Fishman's work, a strong sense of play, of contingency, of the give and take that comes from one painterly decision opening up possible next moves and foreclosing others, that results from her improvisatory, process-driven method of painting—is counterbalanced by the grid, a constant presence in her oeuvre. Fishman's grid functions not so much as a predetermined scaffold but as an always emerging specter: she does not start with the grid; it develops through an intuitive process of mark-making. Every time she makes a move, applies a block of color, or scrapes it down again, a matrix surfaces on her canvas; yet when we try to pin it down, to trace its horizontals and verticals, to see it as a form in and of itself, it disappears and all we can see are those marks, the blocks of color, the scrapings.

Most of her mark-making in *A Little Ramble*, as contingent as it is, whether comprising broad swaths or narrow lines, application or incision, is rectilinear, following the edges of her support. But there are moments—just moments—where something else happens: white paint applied in an arcing stroke in the upper-right corner, or scrubbed into the surface at the top of the greenish patch lower down, or watery dark blues staining the canvas in big blobs. The effect strikes me as akin to the Renaissance technique of sfumato—a softening, a haze, a fog, as if the clouds have descended. A smoky incursion into an otherwise orderly space. A form of mark-making that is also a sort of erasure.

Fishman's painting does and undoes the grid. The paint—like air, like water—cannot be contained, or can, but only provisionally.

■ ■ ■

A Little Ramble—like all of Fishman's paintings made since 2011, the year of her first extended stay on an artist's residency at the Emily Harvey Foundation—is marked by her experience of Venice.[1] Venice signifies for the artist in many ways: she speaks of the algae-mottled plaster and crumbling stone and brick of the walls of the city; the soaring architecture of the churches; the art of Titian and Tintoretto and other masters of the Venetian Renaissance; views of the city painted by the 19th-century English landscapist J.M.W. Turner; the quality of the air and light, which she describes as having an almost physical, substantial presence—she doesn't use the word "ether," but that's the closest analogue; and, of course, the water, which has determined and defined the city's form for centuries and constantly threatens to overwhelm it.

You can find all of these references in Fishman's paintings if you look at them in a certain fashion—the horizontal disposition of many of her rectangular canvases predisposes us to see them as landscapes or cityscapes or seascapes, to read narrative into abstraction. But all these readings-in, it seems to me, speak not to what the paintings *mean*, but to what they *do*. Fishman's recent works enact what might be described as the overwhelming of form by entropy: a city eroding from water and age; *disegno* (drawing—but also rationality, intellectualism, structure—a mark of the Florentine Renaissance) dissolved under the pressure of *colore* (color—but also passion, the organic, emotion—a specialty of the Venetians); the undoing of the underlying subject in Turner's nature studies by his energetic brushwork, his dedication to capturing the play of light and the particularities of atmosphere revealing the world as an abstraction.

■ ■ ■

Fishman's artistic formation included exposure to art and artists at an early age thanks to her mother, Gertrude Fisher-Fishman, and her paternal aunt, Razel Kapustin, both painters who studied at the Barnes Foundation in Merion, Pennsylvania, and spent endless hours at the Philadelphia Museum of Art with young Louise in tow. It continued with her rigorous study of both studio art (painting and sculpture) and of art history at the Tyler School of Art in Elkins Park and then at the University of Illinois, Urbana-Champaign.

By the time she arrived in New York in 1965 she had what she describes as the naïve belief that she would become an Abstract Expressionist. For her, Ab Ex—not just as an approach to painting, but as an ethos—seemed to align with her sense of being on the margins: “I saw all those painters as rogues, outside the normal course of things,” she once said. “I knew by the time I got to art school that I was a lesbian . . . I felt that abstract expressionist work was an appropriate language for me as a queer. It was a hidden language, on the radical fringe, a language appropriate to being separate.”[2] She laughs now at her youthful folly: it didn’t take her long to discover that being part of the New York Ab Ex world would only be possible were she a man or willing to sleep with one.

So she turned her attention for a while to the other dominant artistic language happening in avant-garde circles in New York—minimalism—and began making hard-edged paintings that had as their basic structure the grid. She had experimented with the format in graduate school, thanks to the influence of Al Held's work, which she had seen in the galleries of the Art Institute of Chicago; now in New York, Sol LeWitt and Ellsworth Kelly were added to the mix.

As Fishman gained consciousness of her position as an out queer woman living in a sexist world, she became drawn into the women's liberation movement. However, as with her experience with the Ab Ex crowd, mainstream feminism treated her as an outsider: her queerness (and, in some instances, her status as an artist) kept her at the edges. She tells a story about pushing into a feminist art meeting and suggesting a consciousness-raising exercise, a tool of radical feminist organizing in its early years. Everyone agreed, and greeted other women's testimonies in vocal and supportive ways. When it was her turn, Fishman declared "I am a lesbian and I am a painter." The group fell silent. "I was completely ignored and without missing a beat, they carried on. They didn't know what to do with me," she says now. She found her footing in a specifically lesbian feminism, a radical one, and starting in the later sixties began to meet with a group of artists, writers, and thinkers: during the summer of 1969, she met weekly with Patsy Norvell, Tricia Brown, and Carole Gooden, and come fall of that year, she began meeting with Norvell and a group of Norvell's artist friends, who lived in and around Soho.

It was at this time that Fishman began to see her painting clearly through the lens of her politics. She describes this phase as one of "wanting to get all the male stuff out of my painting"—wanting, that is, to unsee and unlearn what she was now recognizing as an exclusively male history of her chosen medium. Encountering Eva Hesse's work for the first time, she recognized the sculptor's attempt to refashion minimalism by combining its industrial repetition, modular forms, and gridded structures with unconventional materials—string, fiberglass, rubber, etc.—that suggested the body's fragility and capacity for decay. Fishman saw this approach, one based on a material experimentation and formal play, as a clear challenge to the maleness of the avant-garde. Hesse gave Fishman permission, as she tells it, to "do whatever the fuck I wanted"—to be in that very space of outside-ness that her gender, her sexuality, and her political commitments had pushed her, and find a productive home there.

So she began to experiment with new materials and techniques. This period in her work—from roughly 1969 to 1973—was one of undoing: of rejecting painting, at least momentarily, in some cases by literally cutting up her canvases and sewing them back together as combines or collages. The grid was still there, and would continue to be, but it was now no longer Held's grid or LeWitt's grid or Kelly's grid—it was thoroughly and completely her own.

■ ■ ■

In her most recent works, the grid arises in multiple ways, but never claims primacy—in Fishman's nimble hands, almost as soon as it emerges it dissolves under the pressure of color and gesture, making way for a sort of airiness or adding an optical density, by turns.

Piano Nobile (plate 31) is, relatively speaking, fairly completely covered in paint, and yet it respires to an extraordinary degree. The air in Fishman's paintings is not the result of emptiness, of bare canvas showing through between the masses of paint, but is a matter of color, of a sort of openness of touch on the surface, of a certain softening of edges. The painting is composed of blues and blue greens and coppery browns and ochre and red and—unexpectedly, and delightfully—one patch of the purest purple. Fishman also serves us a generous helping of white, which exists both in its own right and as an incursion into the other patches of color, tempering and blending the rectilinear design. *Piano Nobile* is all about layers—the red remains on view despite the dun brown (a non-color, an admixture of too many hues at once) that is painted atop; the blues and grays and olives drip over and through; the drag of a wide spackle knife excavates dried underpainting here, deposits lips of pigment there. The result is almost startlingly sensual—and at one point becomes quite literally tactile, when we see that her fingers have gotten into the act, dragging ultramarine in short strokes in the lower-left quadrant of the canvas. The massing of the colored blocks on the surface seems distinctly architectural—it would not be out of line to see a cityscape in this abstraction (not least because of the title, which refers to the main floor of a palazzo)—but they also seem to signify water and light: all that is solid melts into air, into reflection, into luminosity.

The incursion of the diagonal and the curve, when they happen in Fishman's new paintings, are striking for exactly the reasons you might expect: the careful stasis of the rectilinear becomes dynamic, agitated, and organic by turns. *Mon Semblable Mon Frère* (plate 41) is a case in point. The grid is now twisted, so that it maps a vertiginous, canted, three-dimensional space despite sitting resolutely on the surface of its rectangular support. The canvas is smaller than usual, a narrow vertical, and the palette is somber—dark blues, burnt sienna, umbers, reds, with the leavening effect of a transparent sky blue at points. Fishman speaks of the soaring spaces of churches in relation to some of her recent work; to me there is something more urgent and more driving about *Mon Semblable Mon Frère* than that. This is no sanctuary. It is the city as revealed by Aleksandr Rodchenko's or Laszlo Moholy-Nagy's constructivist photography—made strange, turned into an abstraction, thanks to the handheld camera's capacity to look at the world askew, from above and below and sideways. This same energy is apparent in *Cadence* (plate 46), a larger canvas whose structure likewise depends on oblique angles and a heavy scaffold. But here, because of the scale of the canvas, it is less photography that is at issue than the slashing, energetic, even athletic brushwork of Franz Kline, one of Fishman's early and most significant influences.

The title, *Mon Semblable Mon Frère* ("my likeness, my brother") comes from the preface to *Les Fleurs Du Mal* by the French poet Charles Baudelaire—who called out his readers ("Hypocrite reader, my likeness, my brother!") for not recognizing that the immorality that his poetry was judged to enact, which led to its censoring, was simply a reflection of the world, and thus was theirs, too. It was an accusation subsequently quoted by T.S. Eliot in *The Wasteland*—a lament about the disintegration, decay, and dissolution of the modern city. Here is where entropy gives way to something more sinister—degeneration, a cultural malaise, a decadence. This painting contains precisely that pathos.

And look how Fishman manages to eke out this pathos—but now, in a more brittle form, one that comes from eyes that have seen it all—in a painting whose palette is reduced to black and white. As we looked at *Sharps and Flats* (plate 44) together, the artist said she'd given it a boring title. It seemed out of sync, she said, with the jagged, jangly effect of the whole: strong horizontal groundlines that run across the middle register of the canvas, countered by strong, vertical, punctuating marks, some of which veer off on an angle, adding a sort of velocity to the composition. But even if Fishman doesn't recognize her own poetry, her viewers can revel in it: think of the way the words "sharps" and "flats" roll around on your tongue, the spitted "p" of one and "ts" of the other; think of the musical effects of sharp and flat tones—pathos and bathos by turn, dissonance and melancholy.

The curve was not a natural part of Fishman's repertoire; it was something she had to learn (or relearn), in recent years. When it appears—as it does, spectacularly, in *San Stae* (plate 47)—we are reminded again of the athleticism of her method: the way in which each of the marks on her large canvases—rectilinear or not—is made by a body reaching across a surface as big or bigger than her span. Fishman was a basketball player in her teens, and that experience continues to inform how she thinks of the act of painting: the basketball court as an analogue for the rectangle of the support, the tactical and intuitive movements that allow her to react to what has happened and anticipate her next move, and the sheer physicality of wielding her tools across an expansive surface are somehow connected to this latent muscle memory.

Where other painters might imagine the grid as an external structure, projected onto the canvas or the world to allow the viewer to make sense of it as other to themselves, a way to map a space *out there*—Rosalind Krauss famously described it as "antinatural, antimimetic, antireal"[3]—Fishman operates from *within* the grid, just as she operated in the basketball court. It becomes a product and an extension of her body, rather than a predetermined given, and she makes it and unmakes it from within. On her terms.

1. In addition to extensive conversations with Louise Fishman and Ingrid Nyeboe in April and May 2017, I relied on a few excellent texts on Fishman's artistic evolution in preparation of this essay. These included the essays in: Helaine Posner, ed., *Louise Fishman*, exh. cat. (New York: DelMonico Books/Prestel, 2016), especially that by Helaine Posner ("Louise Fishman: The Energy in the Rectangle," 11–21); and an interview with Sharon Butler published in *The Brooklyn Rail*, October 4, 2012.
2. Louise Fishman in Holland Cotter, "Art after Stonewall: Twelve Artists Interviewed—Louise Fishman," *Art in America* 82, no. 6 (June 1994): 59–60. Quoted in Posner, "Louise Fishman: The Energy in the Rectangle," 12.
3. Rosalind Krauss, "Grids," in *Originality of the Avant-Garde and Other Modernist Myths* (Cambridge, MA and London: MIT Press, 1986), 8–22. Originally published in *October* 9 (Summer 1979).

1. The Bread of Time 2016 oil on linen 66 x 39 in 167.6 x 99.1 cm

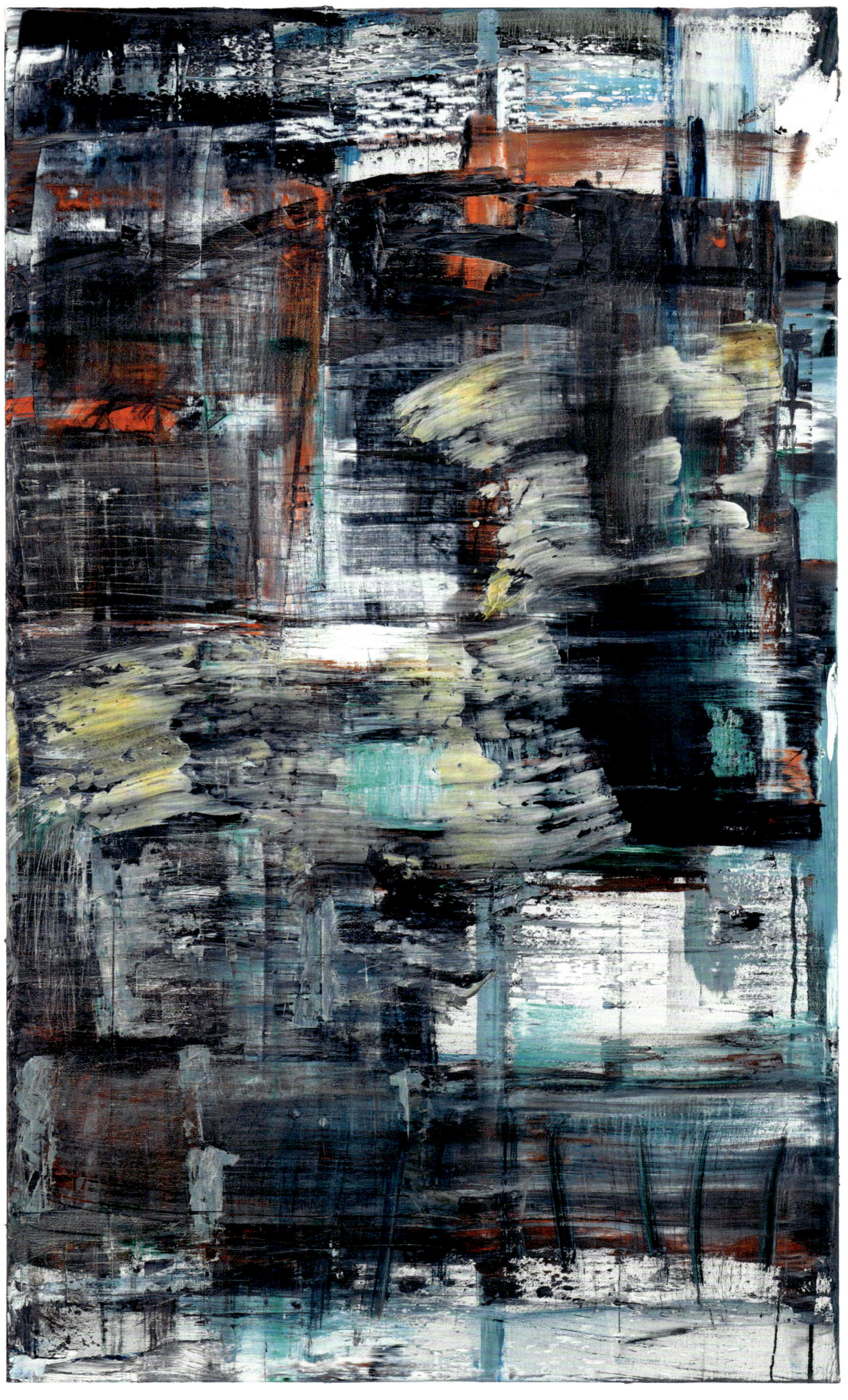

2. Untitled 2016 watercolor and egg tempera on paper 7 7/8 x 7 7/8 in 20 x 20 cm

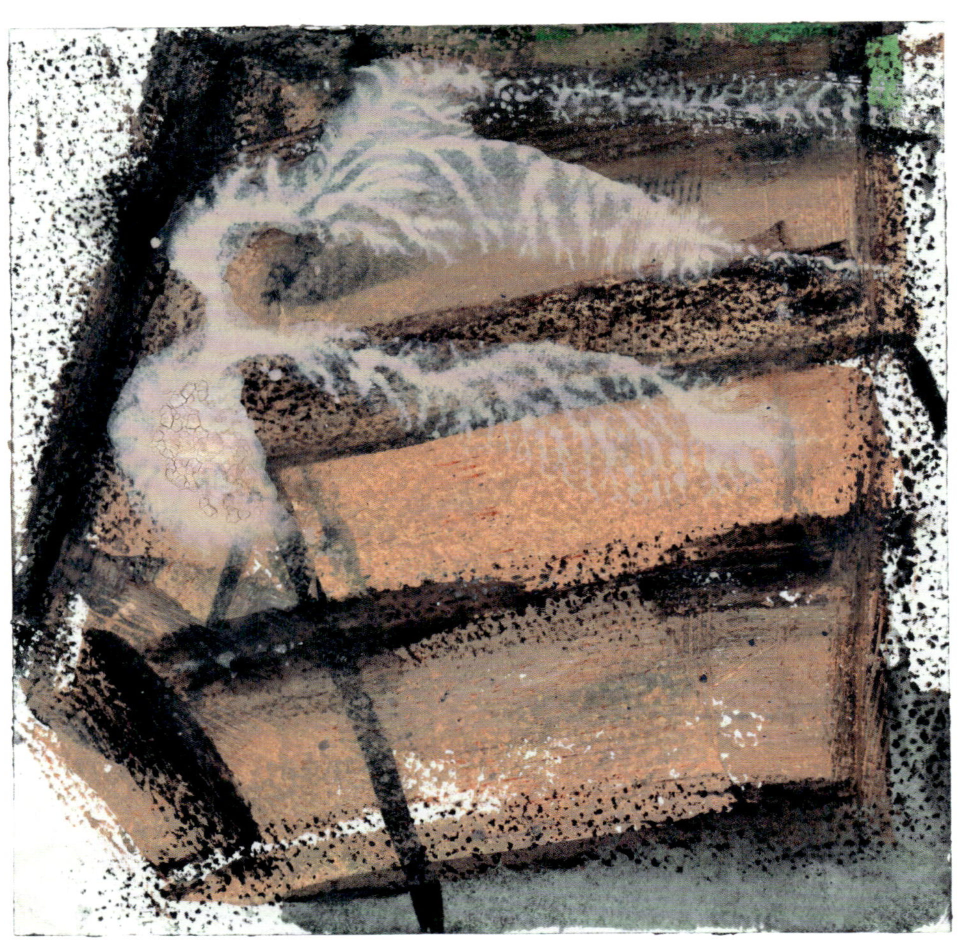

3. Lament 2016 oil on linen 66 x 55 in 167.6 x 139.7 cm

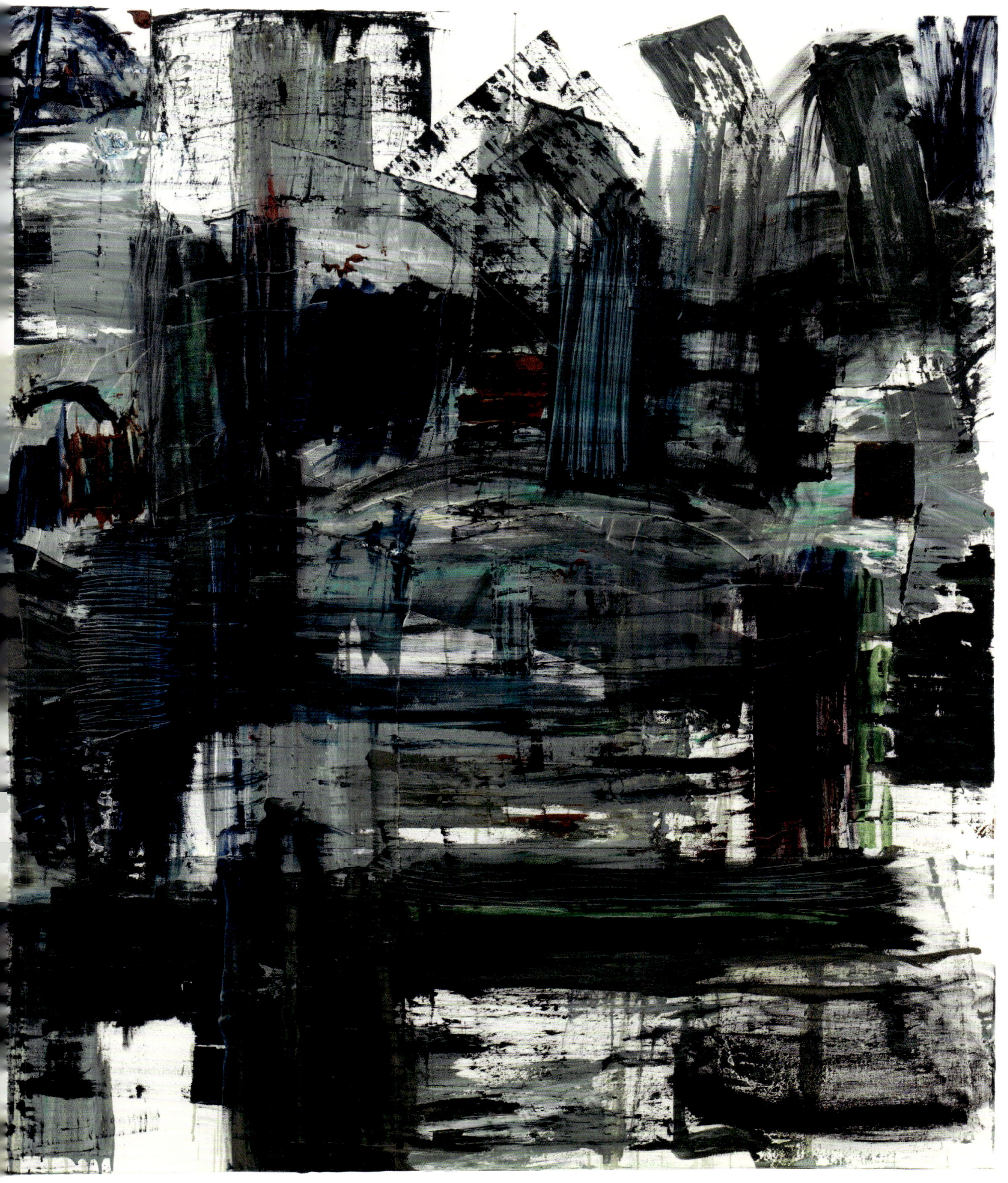

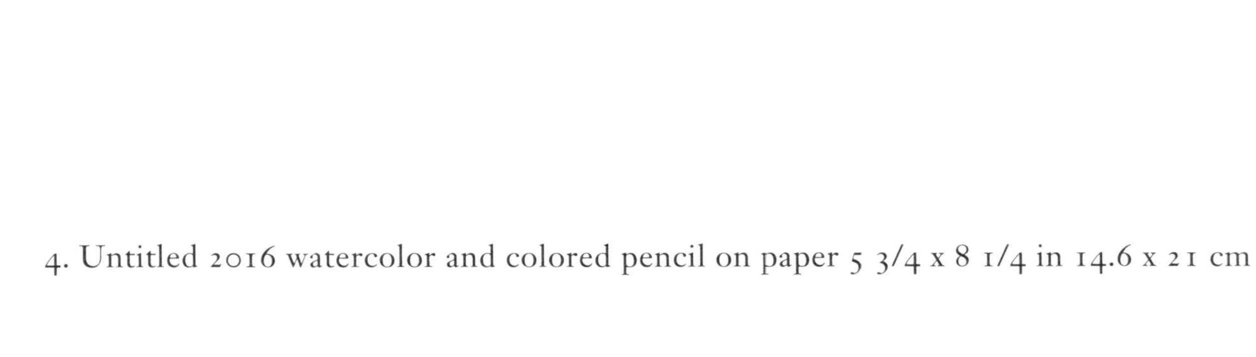

4. Untitled 2016 watercolor and colored pencil on paper 5 3/4 x 8 1/4 in 14.6 x 21 cm

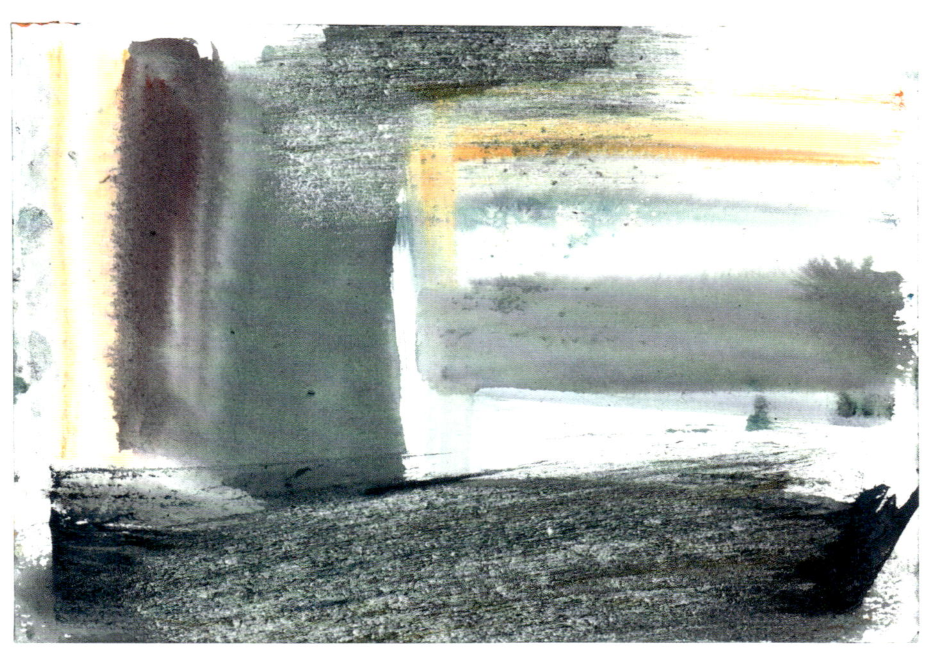

5. Jasper 2016 oil on canvas 30 1/4 x 30 in 76.8 x 76.2 cm

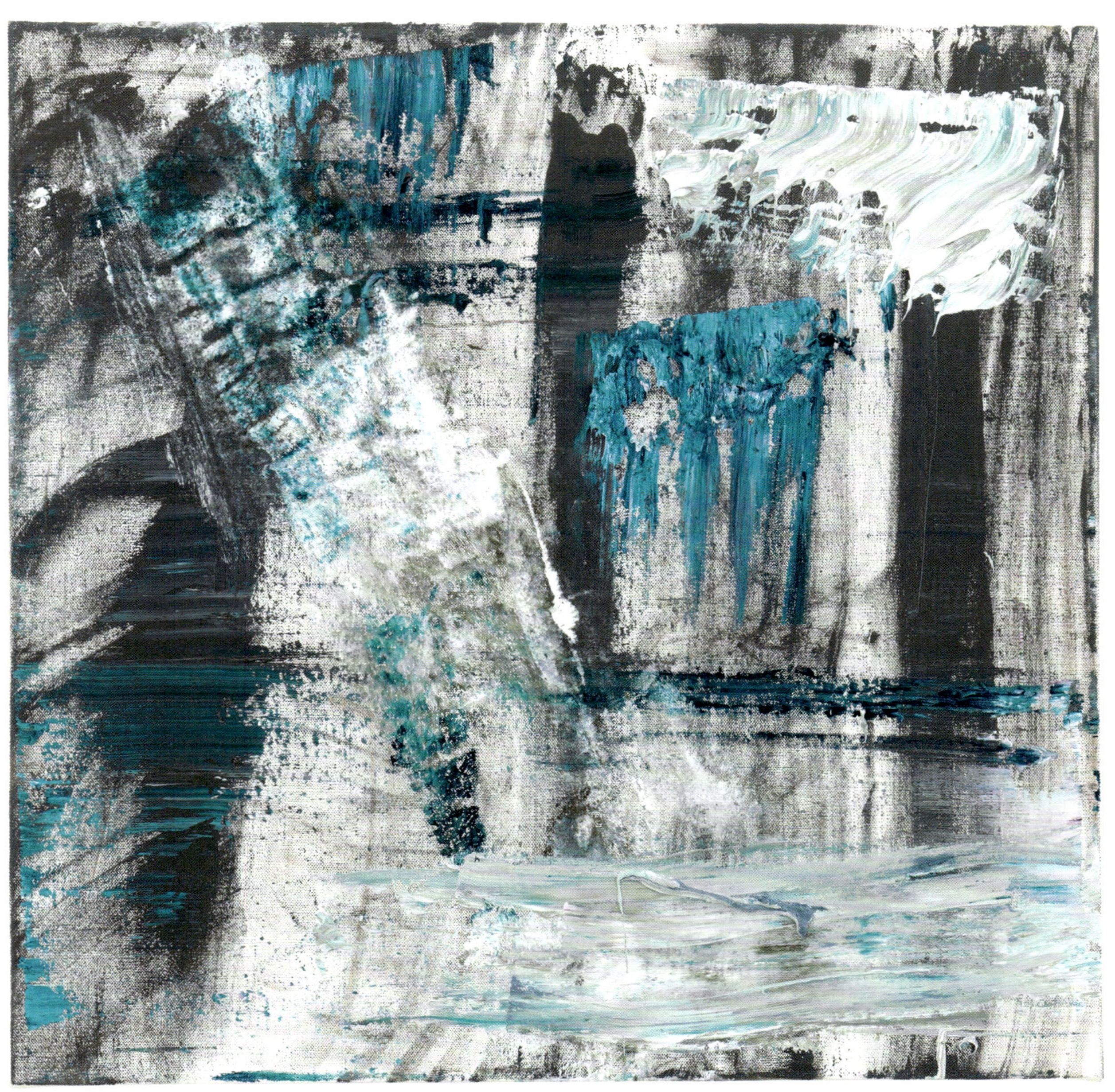

6. Untitled 2016 ink and wash on paper 7 7/8 x 7 7/8 in 20 x 20 cm

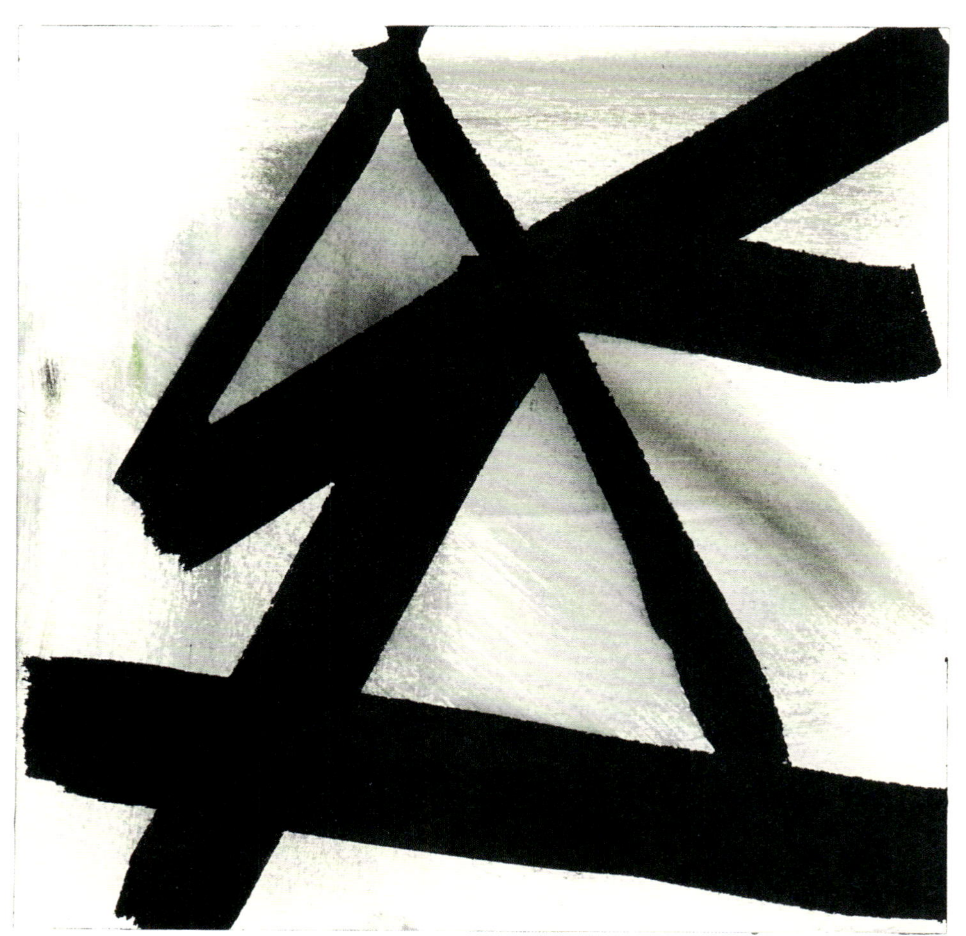

7. Wings of Night 2016 oil on linen 66 x 39 in 167.6 x 99.1 cm

8. Untitled 2016 watercolor and colored pencil on paper 7 x 10 1/4 in 17.8 x 26 cm

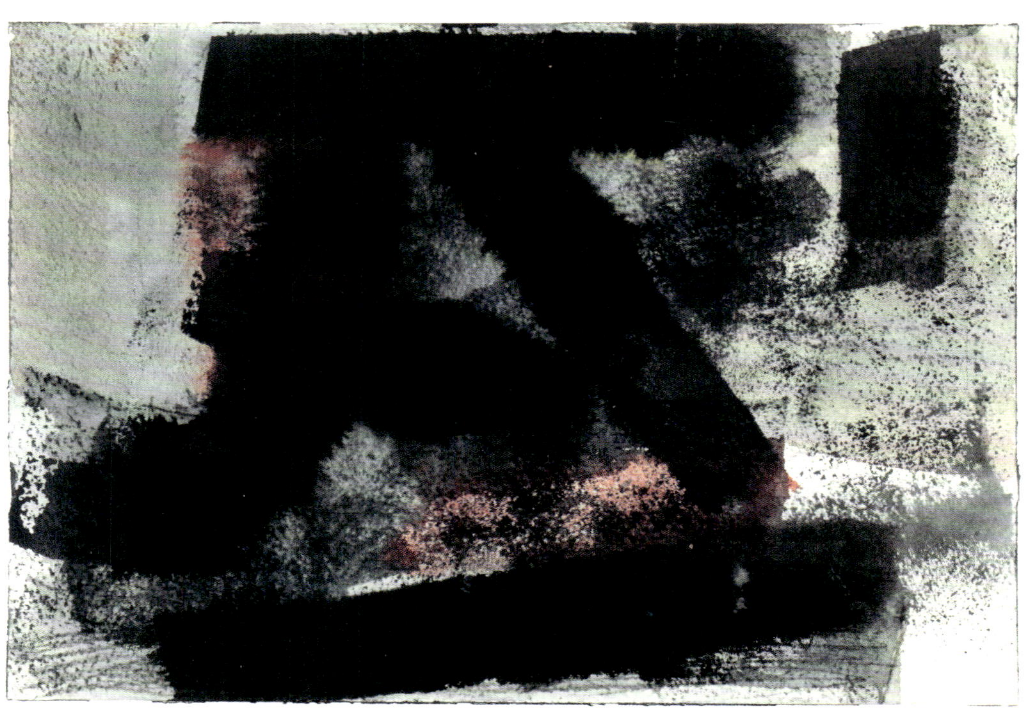

9. Zero 2016 oil on linen 74 x 88 in 188 x 223.5 cm

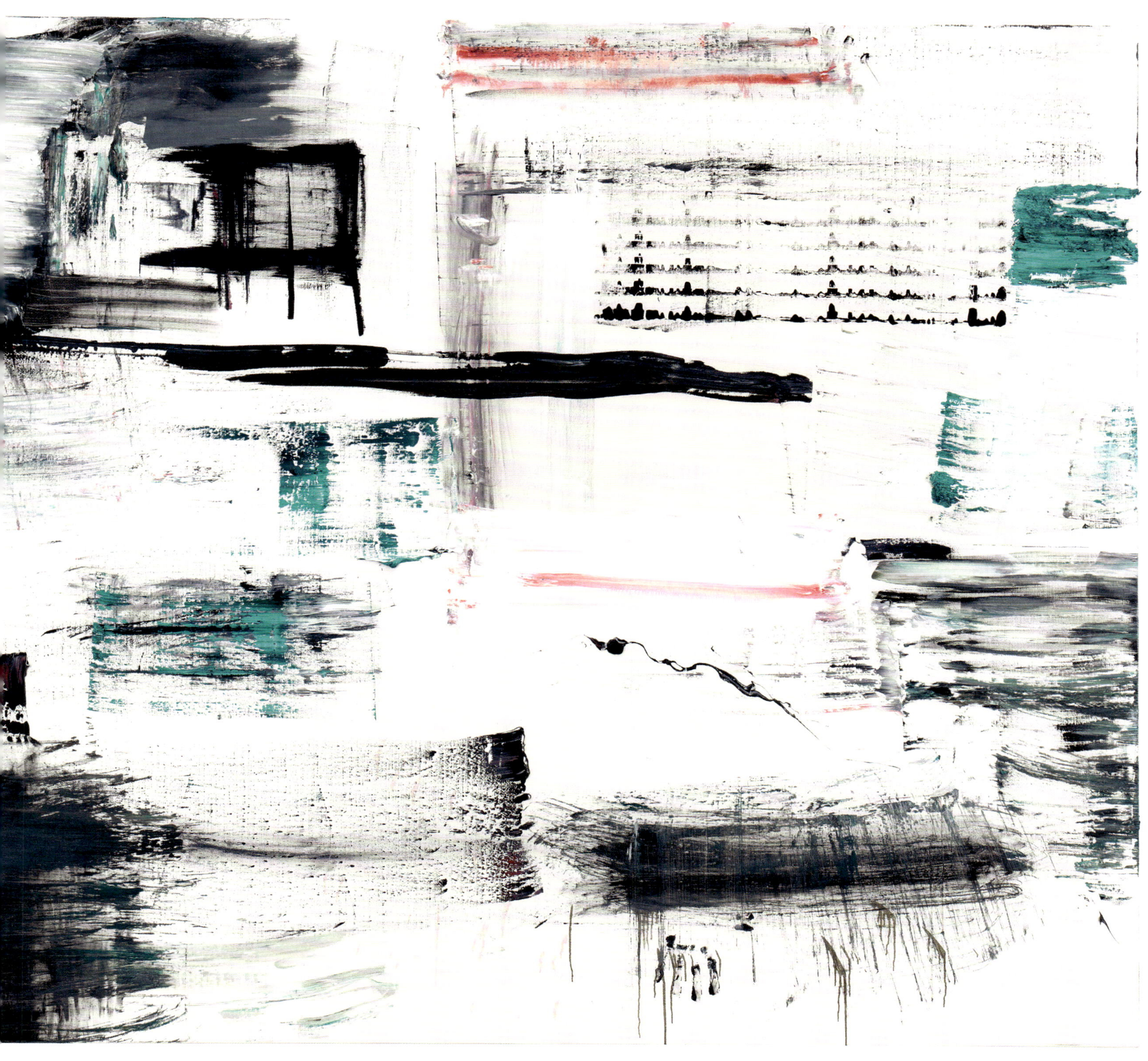

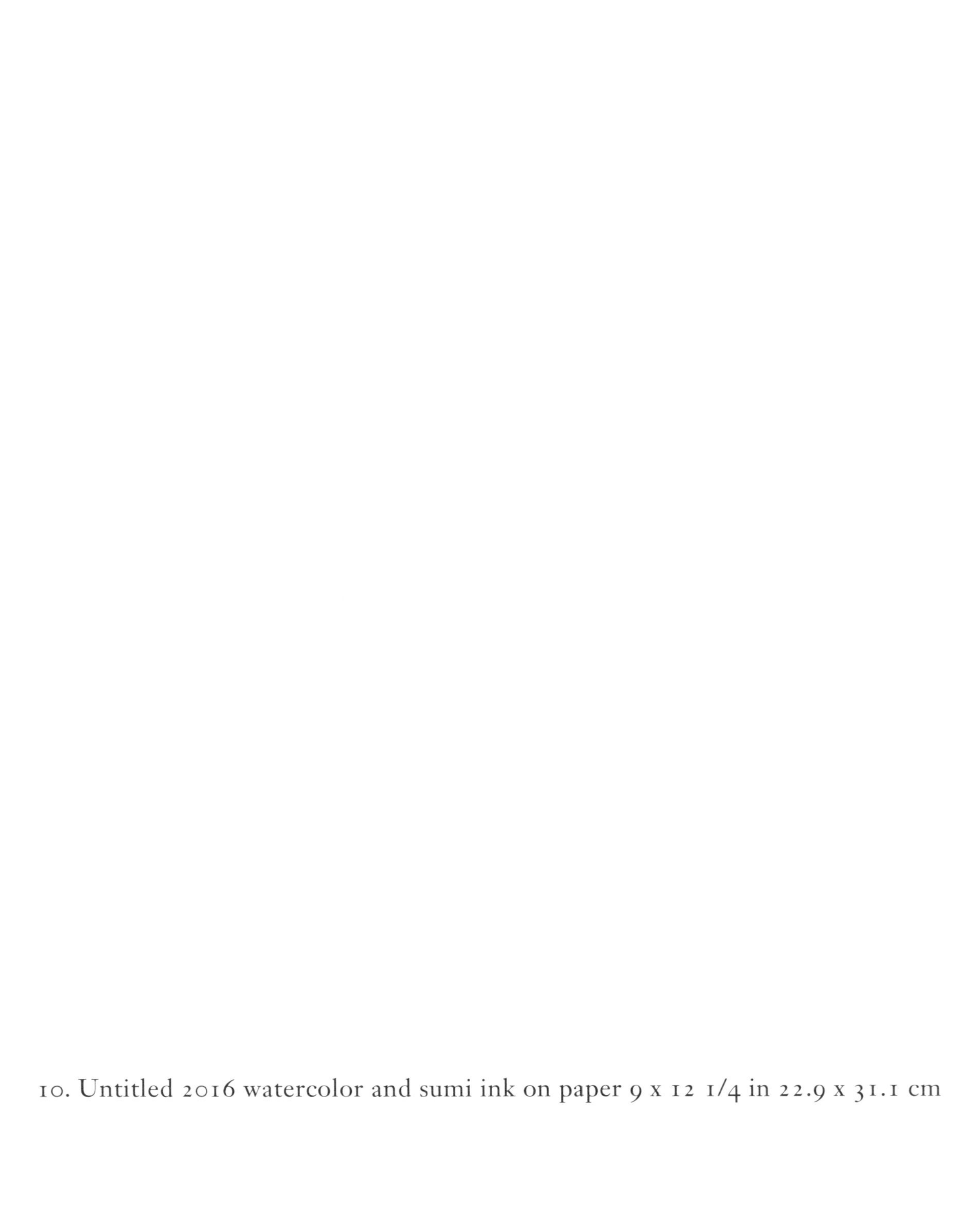

10. Untitled 2016 watercolor and sumi ink on paper 9 x 12 1/4 in 22.9 x 31.1 cm

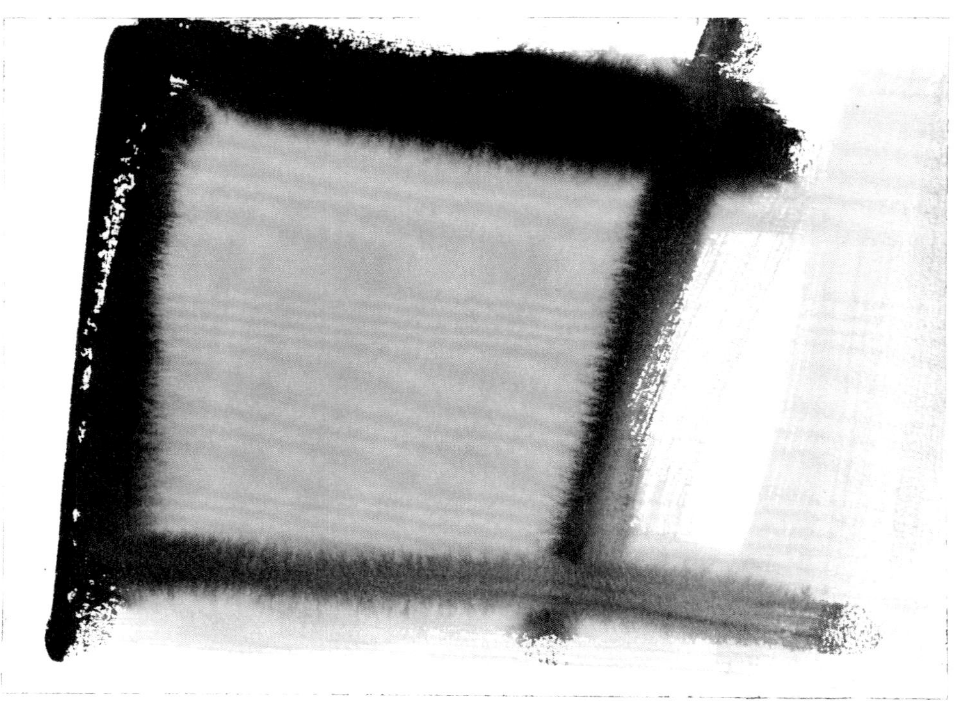

11. One Foot in the River 2016 oil on linen 74 x 86 in 188 x 218.4 cm

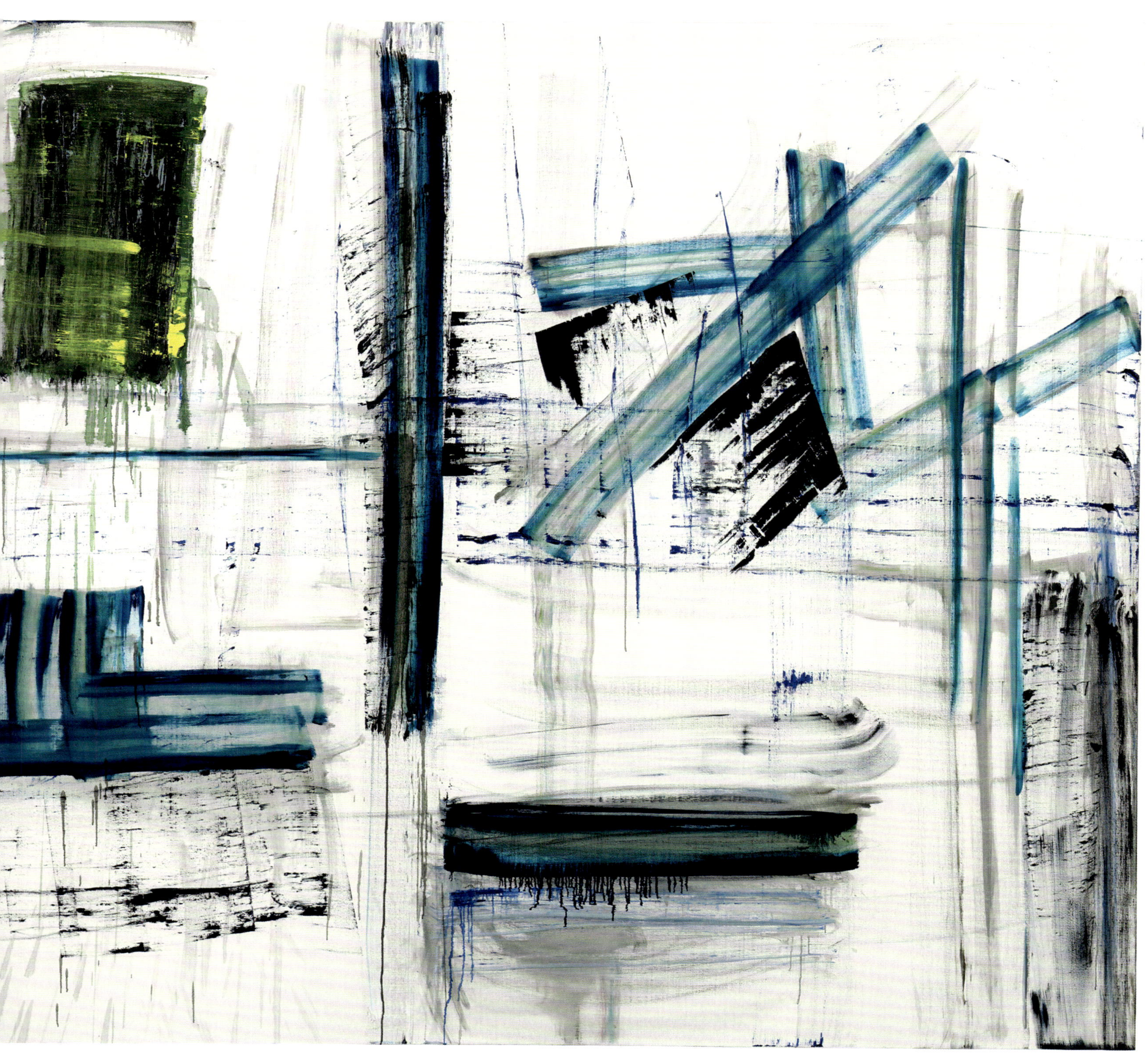

12. Untitled 2016 egg tempera and colored pencil on paper 7 x 10 1/4 in 17.8 x 26 cm

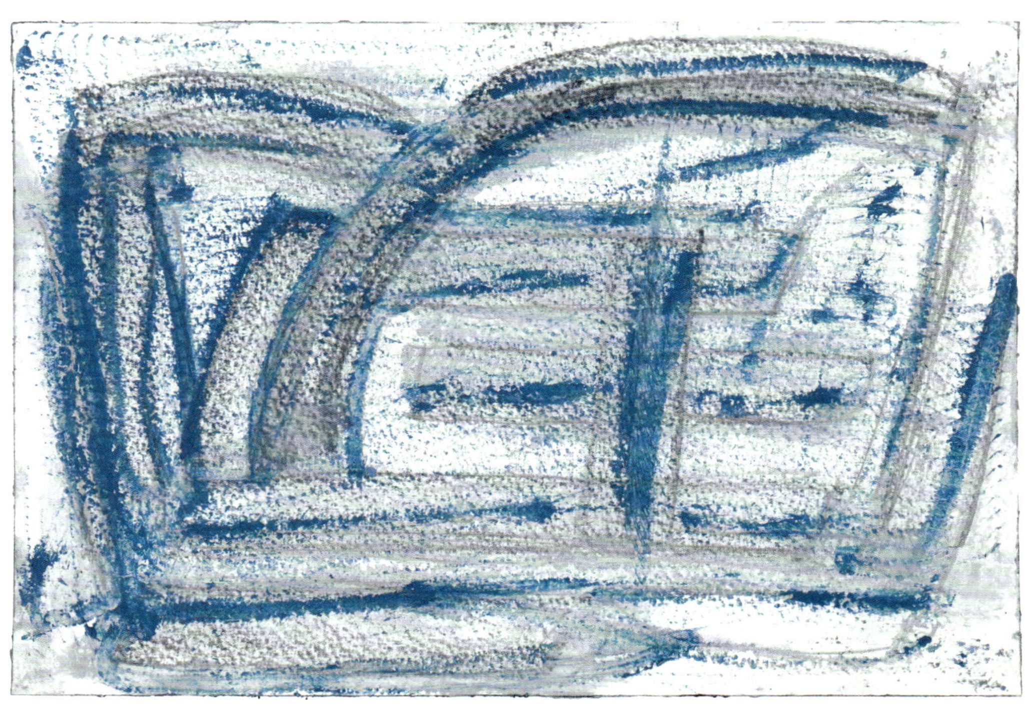

13. Wave on Wave 2016 oil on linen 66 x 39 in 167.6 x 99.1 cm

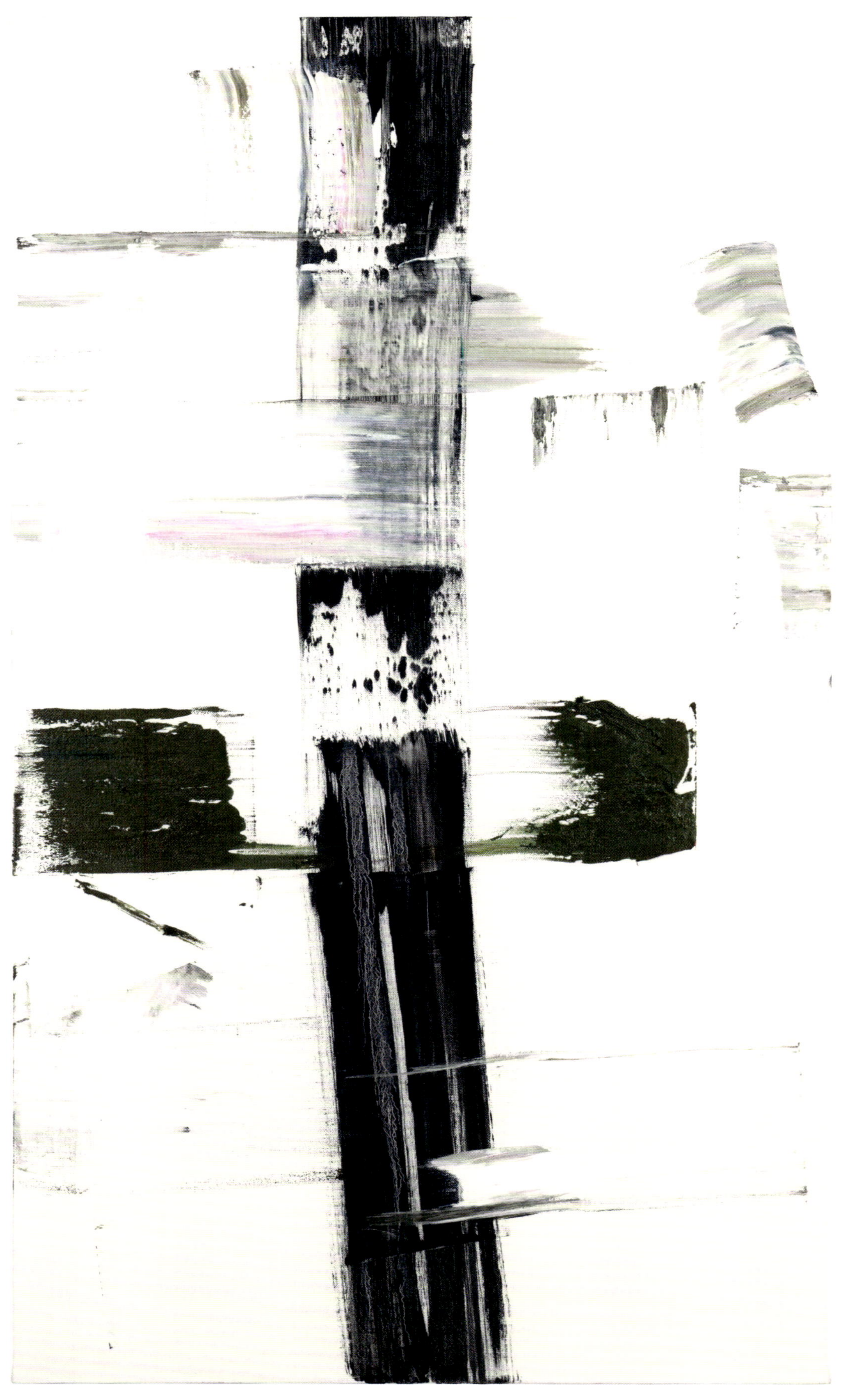

14. Untitled 2016 watercolor and colored pencil on paper 9 x 12 1/4 in 22.9 x 31.1 cm

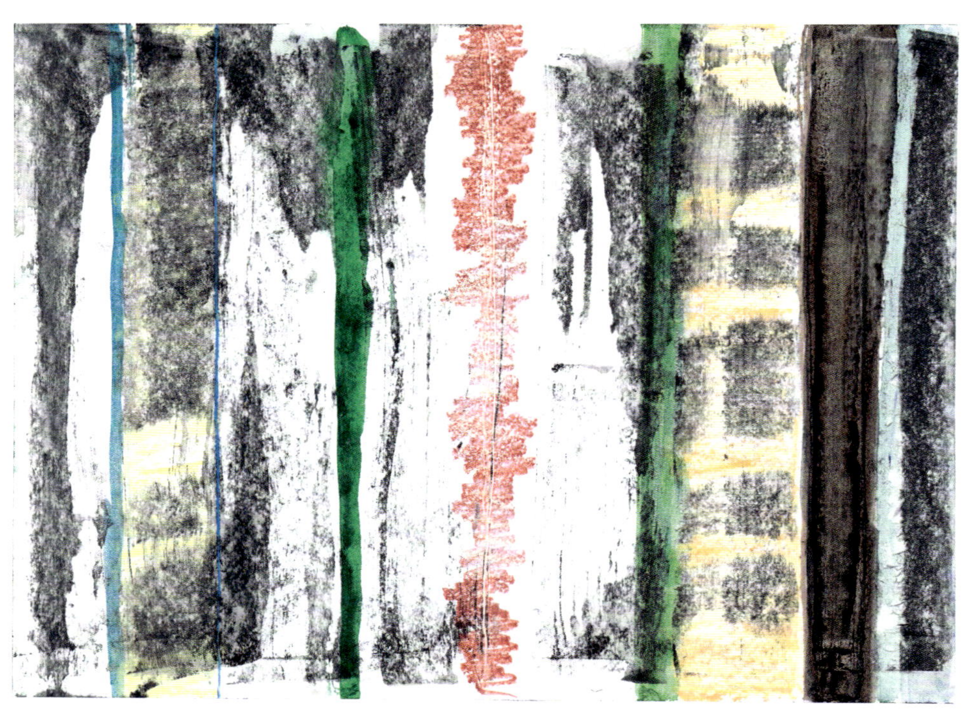

15. Arresø 2016 oil on linen 66 x 39 in 167.6 x 99.1 cm

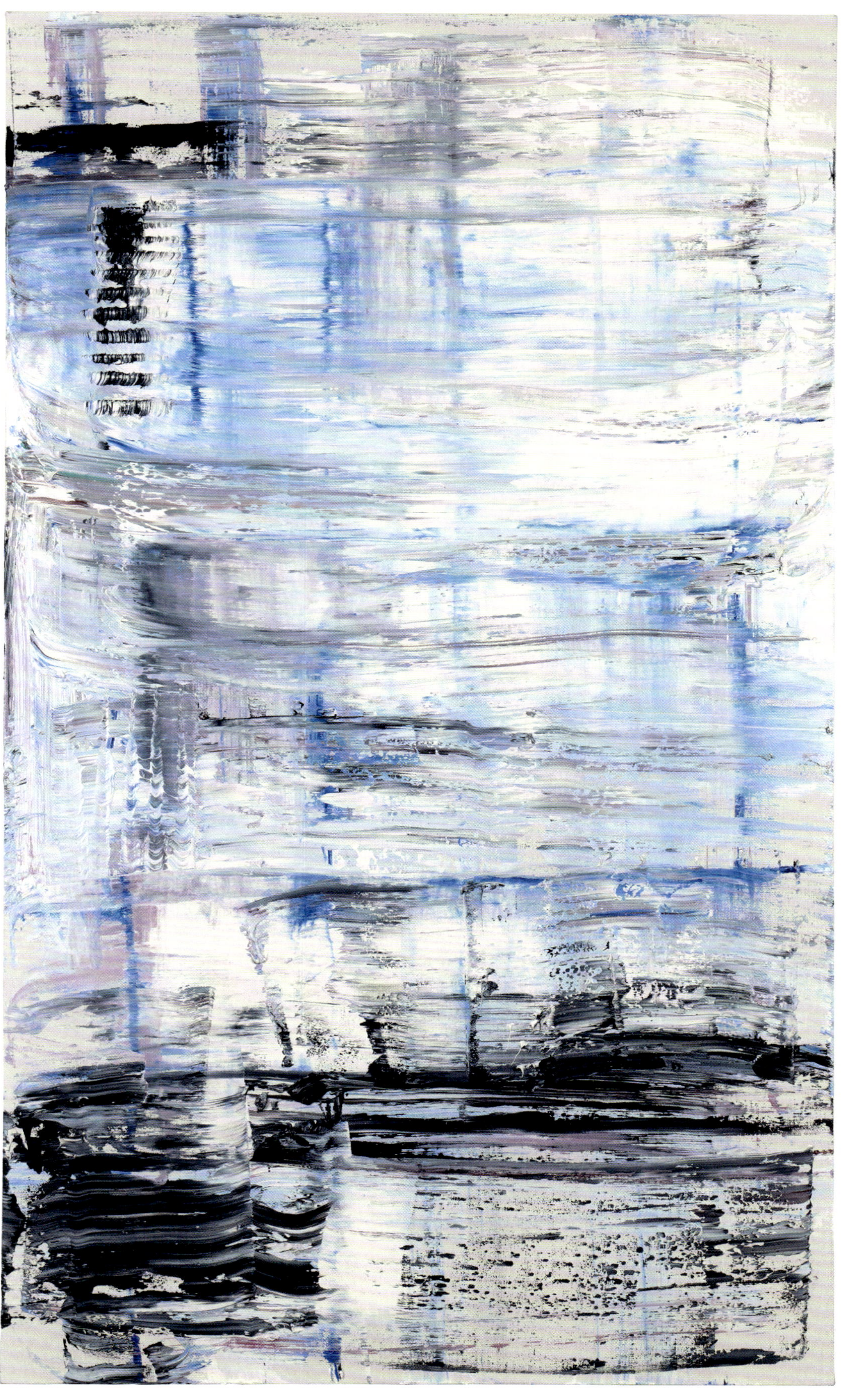

16. Untitled 2016 egg tempera and ink on paper 12 1/2 x 17 3/4 in 31.8 x 45.1 cm

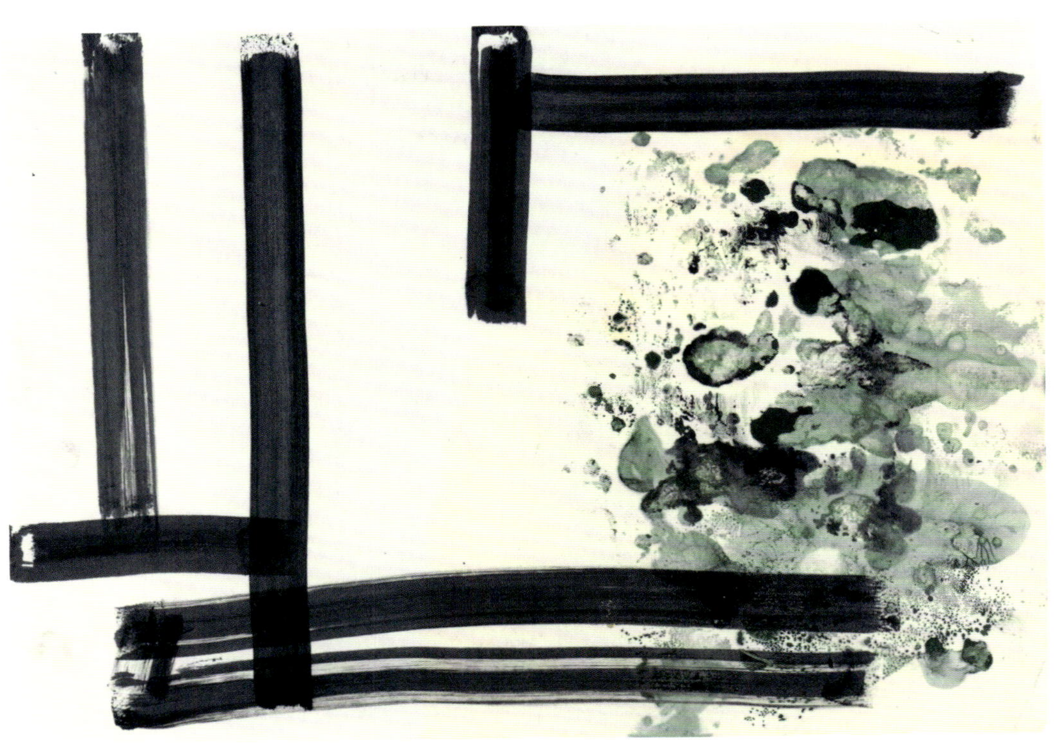

17. Keriah 2016 oil on linen 50 x 30 in 127 x 76.2 cm

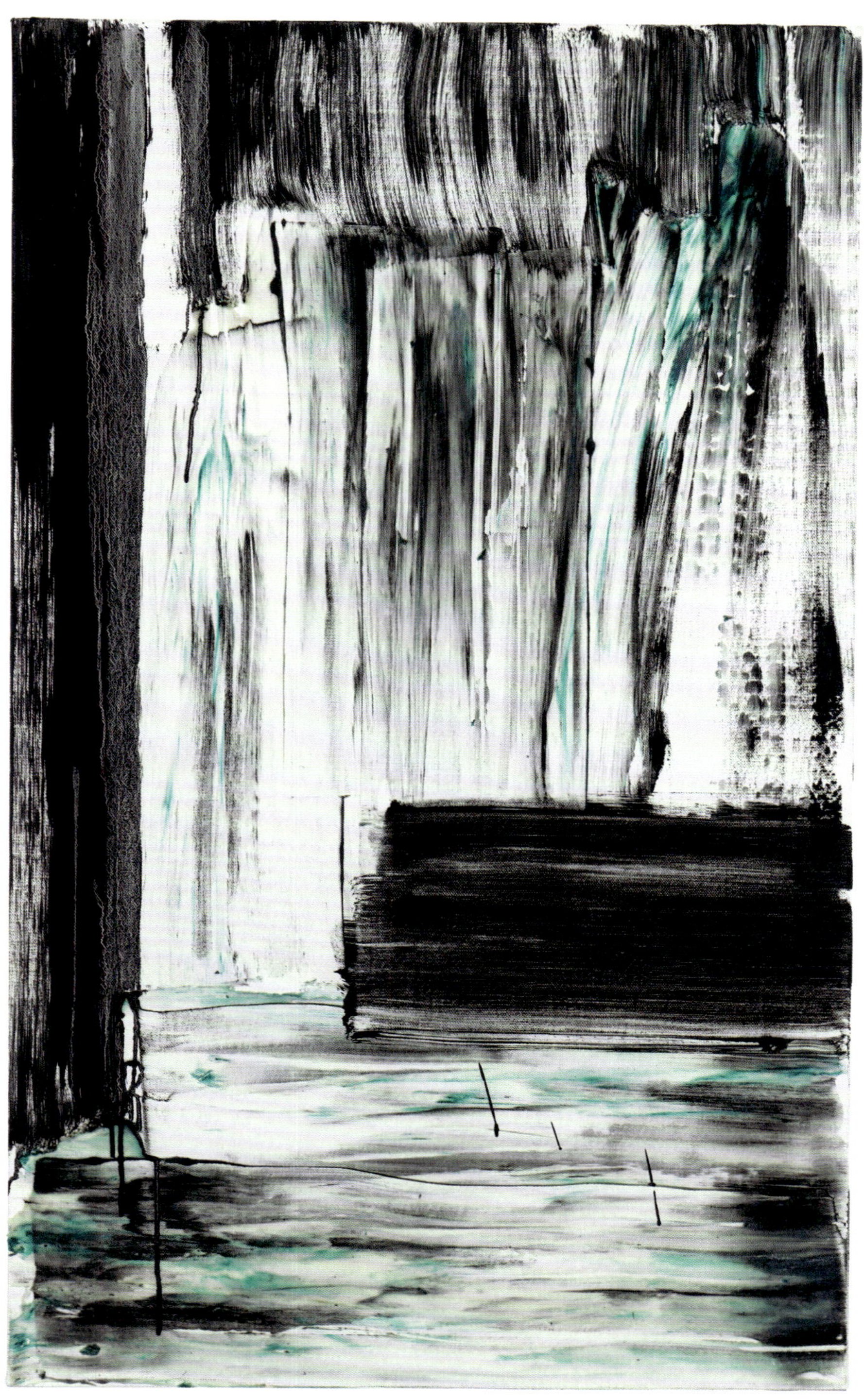

18. Untitled 2016 watercolor and ink on paper 8 1/4 x 5 3/4 in 21 x 14.6 cm

19. The Pinnacles Frisson 2016 oil on linen 60 x 50 in 152.4 x 127 cm

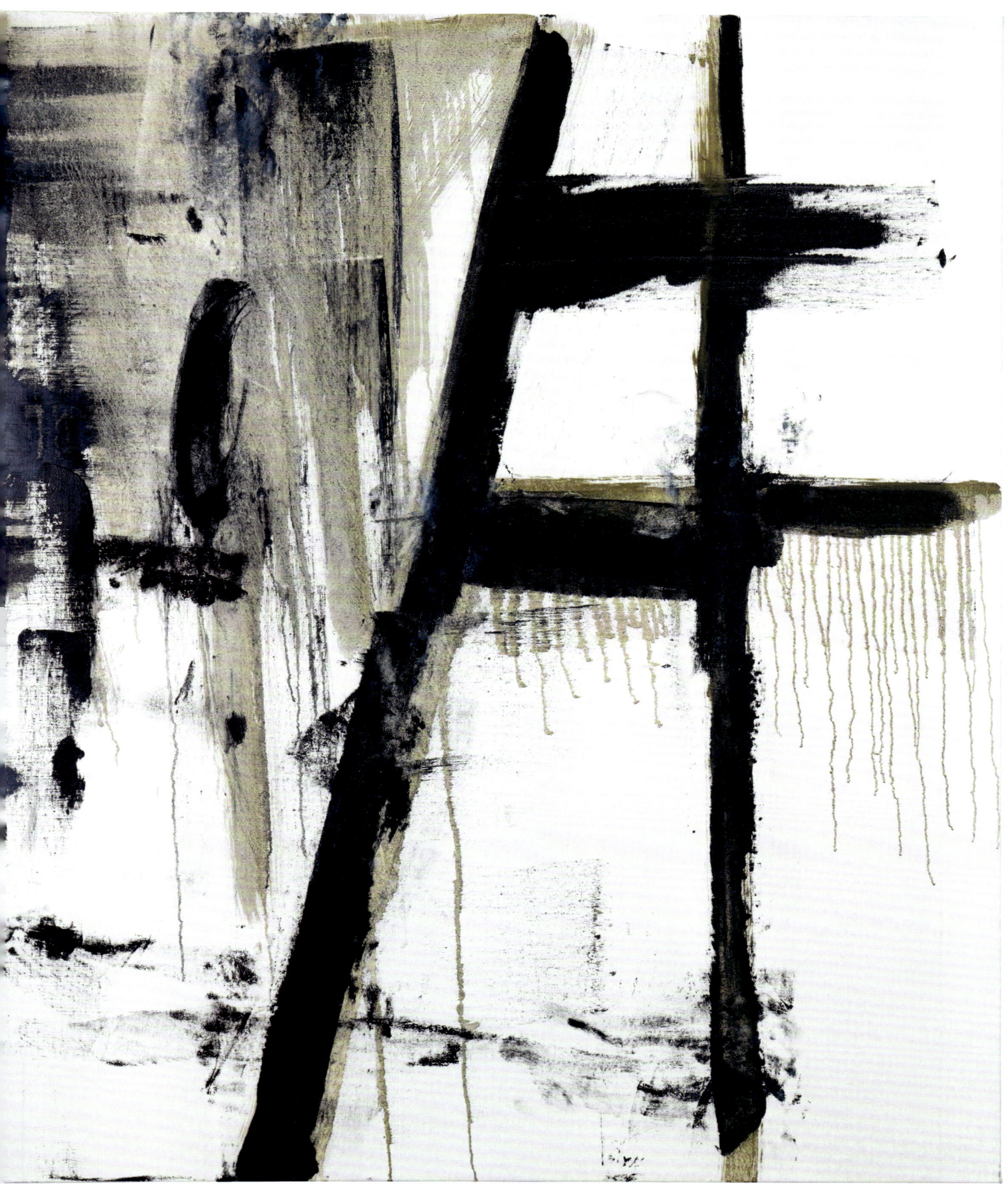

20. Untitled 2016 watercolor and ink on paper 9 x 12 1/4 in 22.9 x 31.1 cm

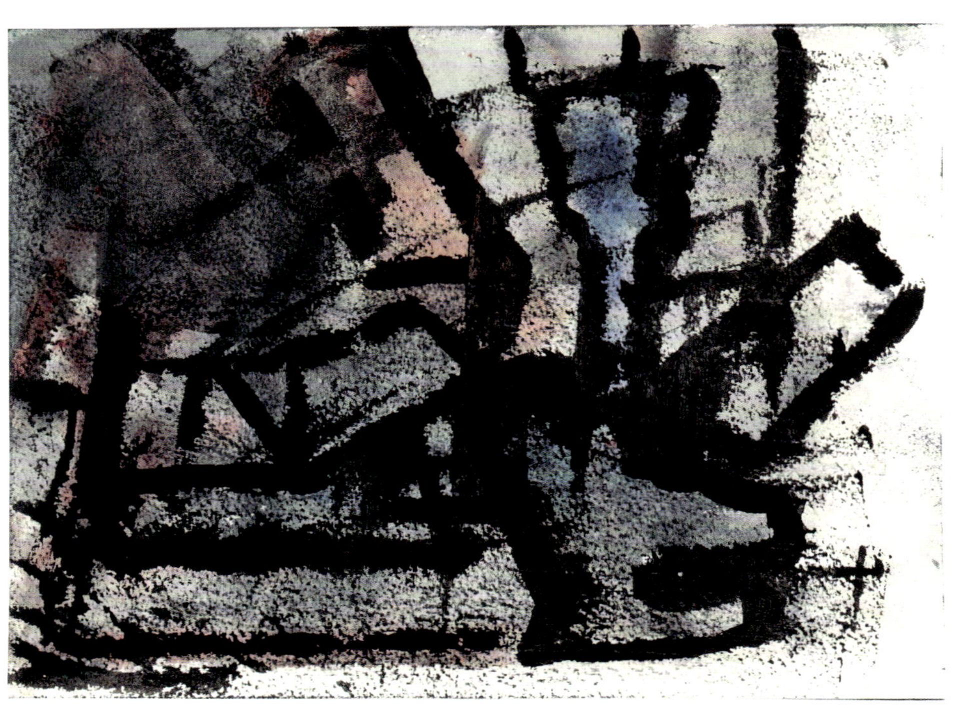

21. Träumerei 2016 oil on linen 70 x 88 in 177.8 x 223.5 cm

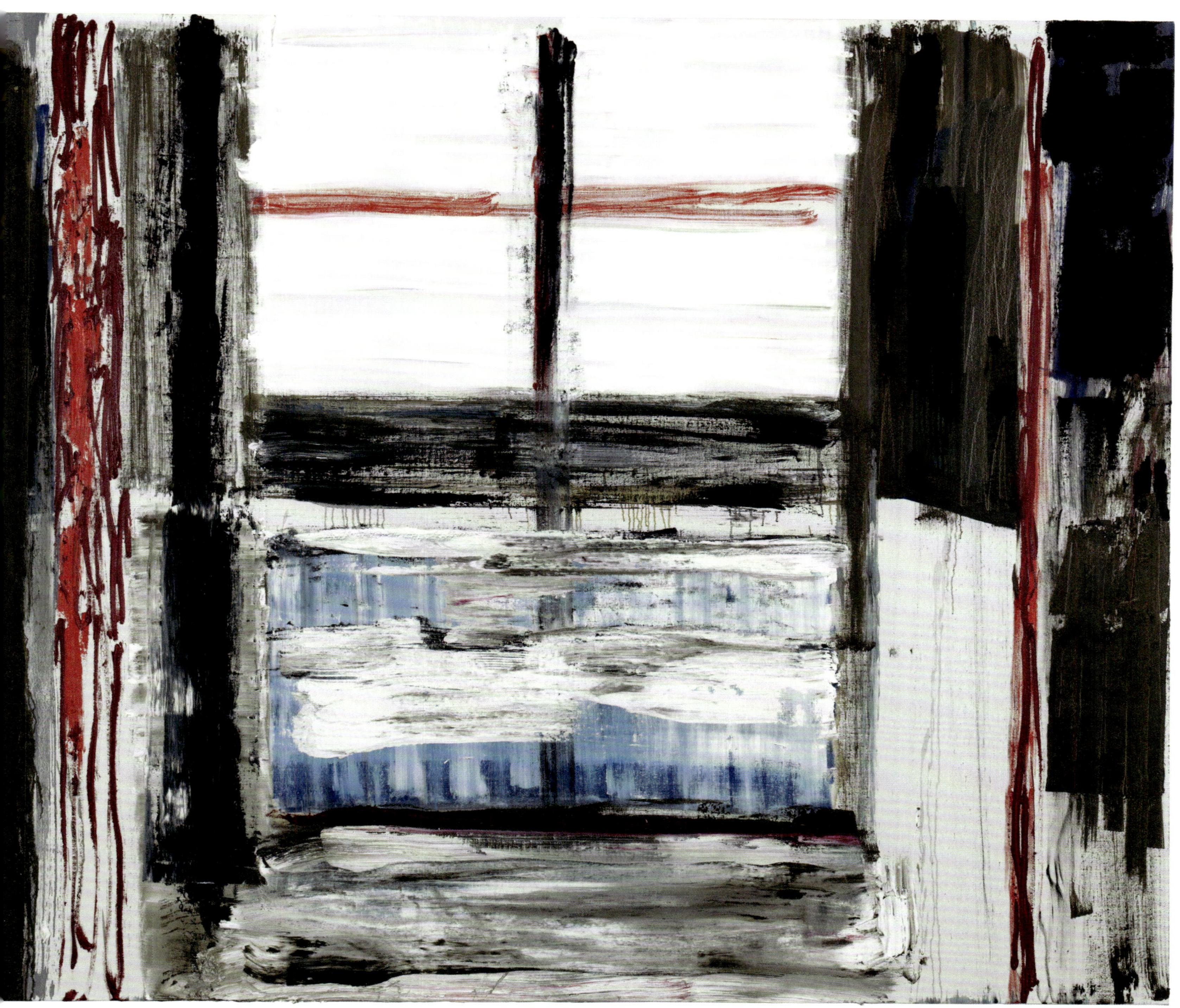

22. Untitled 2016 egg tempera and ink on paper 7 x 10 1/4 in 17.8 x 26 cm

23. There Comes a Warning Like a Spy 2017 oil on linen 72 x 96 in 182.9 x 243.8 cm

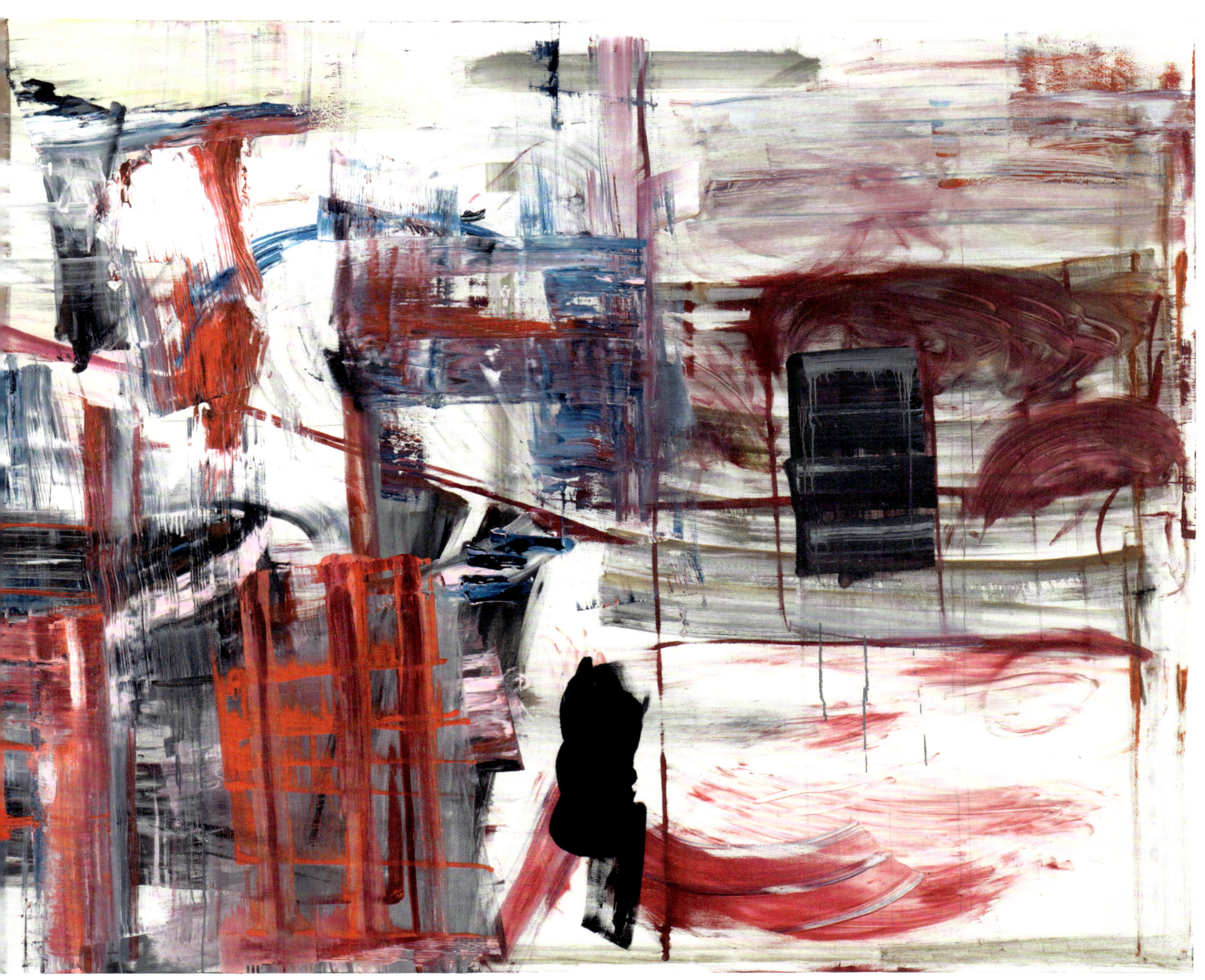

24. Untitled 2016 watercolor on paper 4 x 6 in 10.2 x 15.2 cm

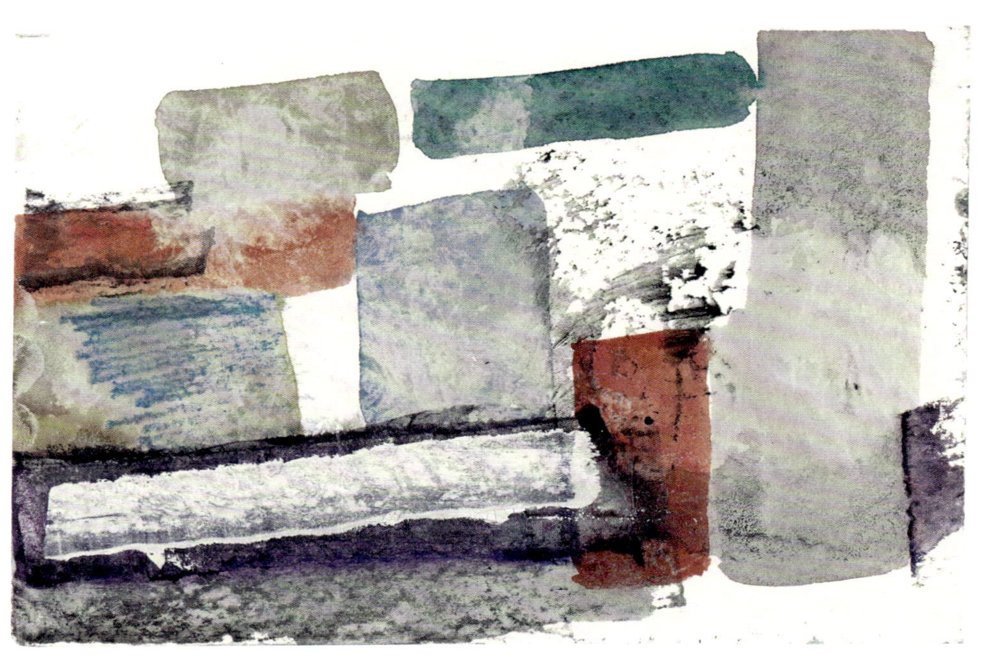

25. A Little Ramble 2017 oil on linen 70 x 90 in 177.8 x 228.6 cm

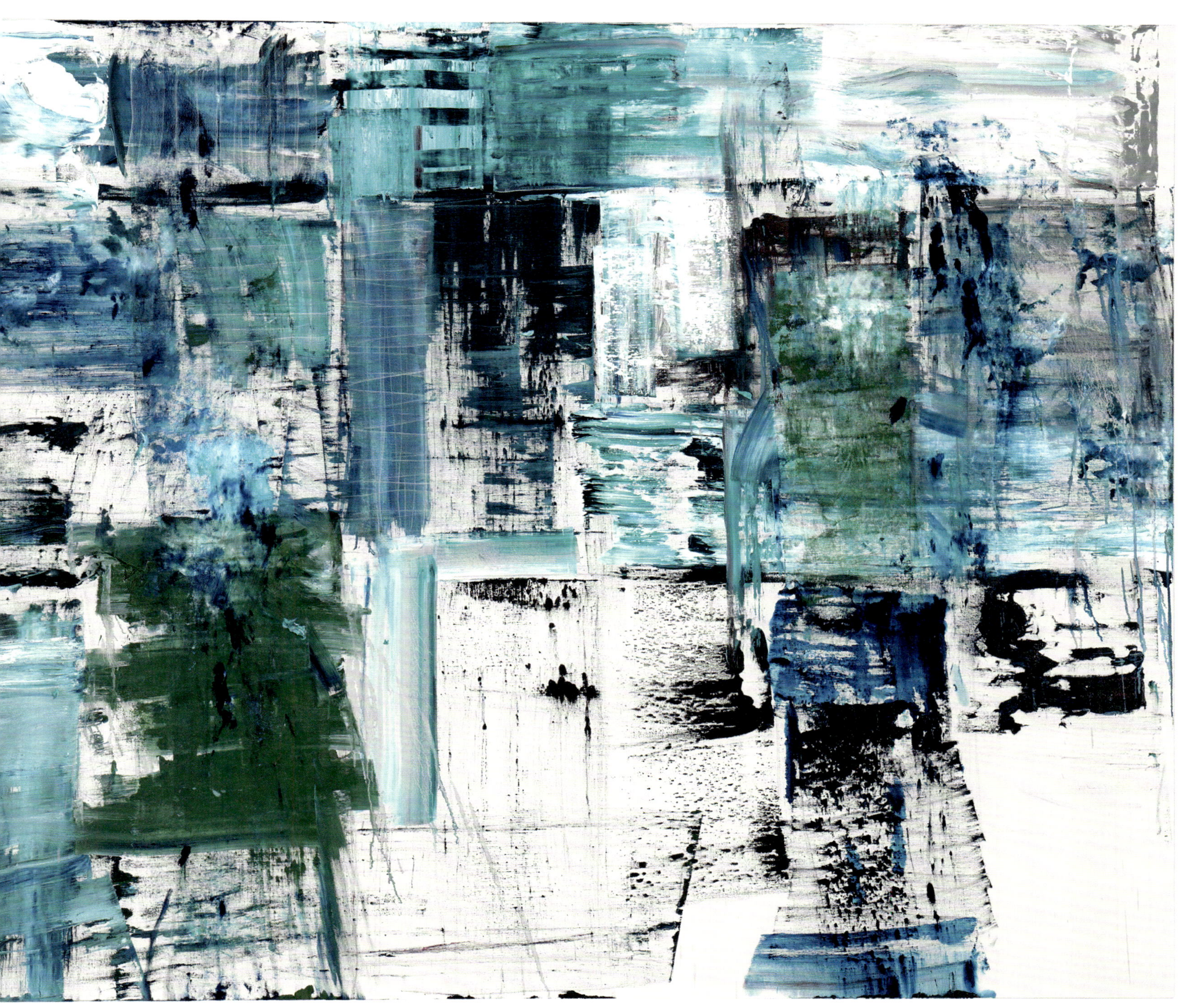

26. Untitled 2016 watercolor and ink on paper 9 x 12 1/4 in 22.9 x 31.1 cm

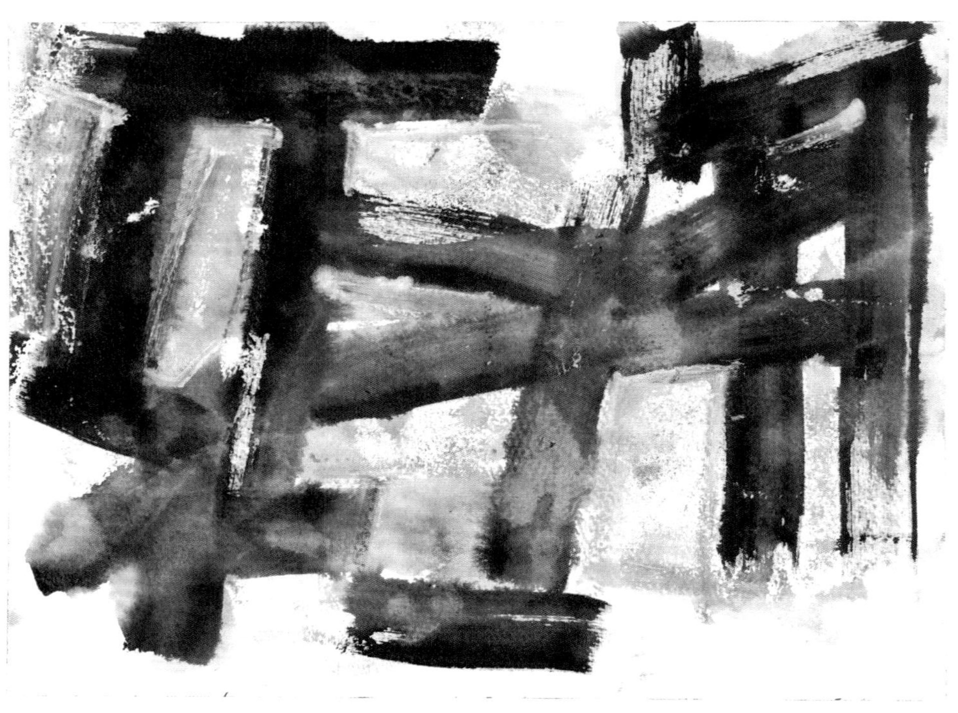

27. Ash, Needle, Pencil, and Match 2017 oil on linen 66 x 55 in 167.6 x 139.7 cm

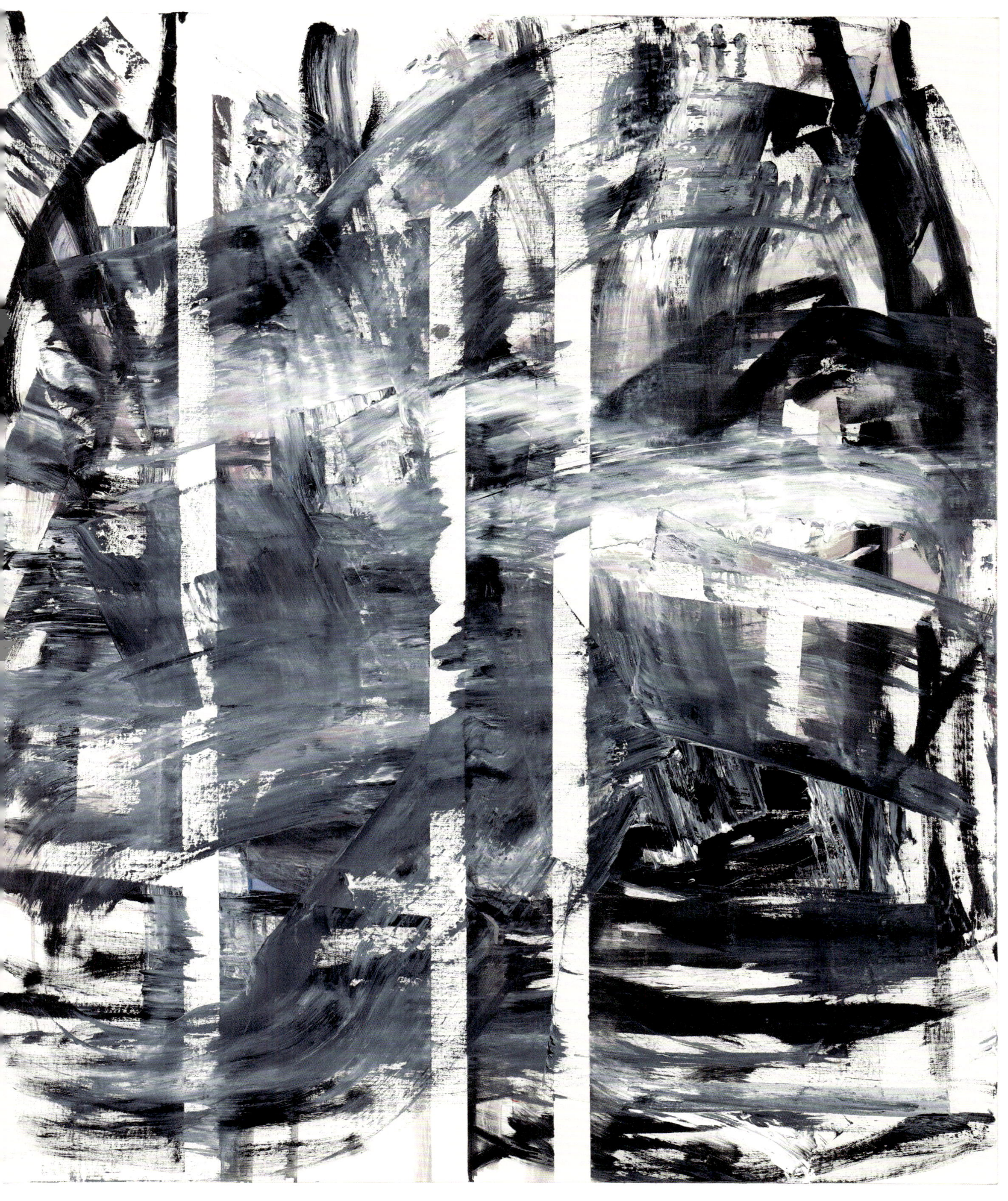

28. Untitled 2016 watercolor, ink, and colored pencil on paper 9 x 12 1/4 in 22.9 x 31.1 cm

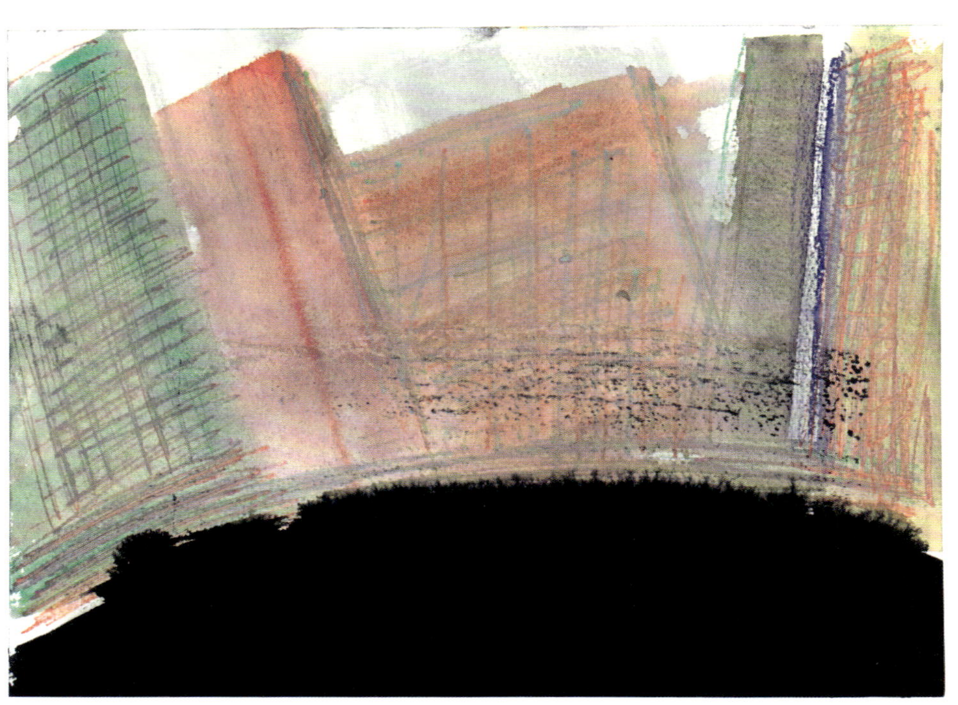

29. Page from a Diary 2017 oil on linen 50 x 30 in 127 x 76.2 cm

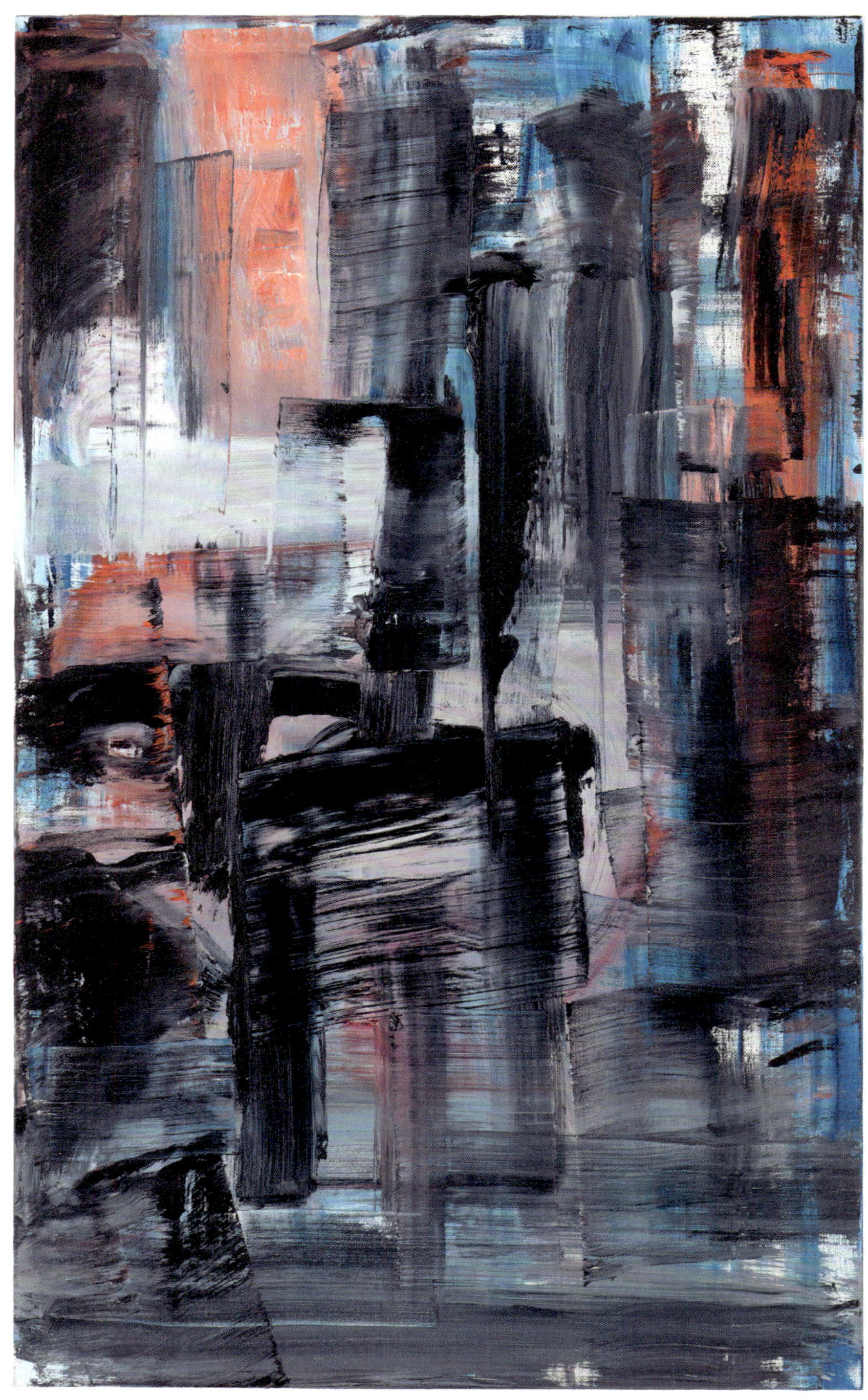

30. Untitled 2016 watercolor and pencil on paper 4 x 6 in 10.2 x 15.2 cm

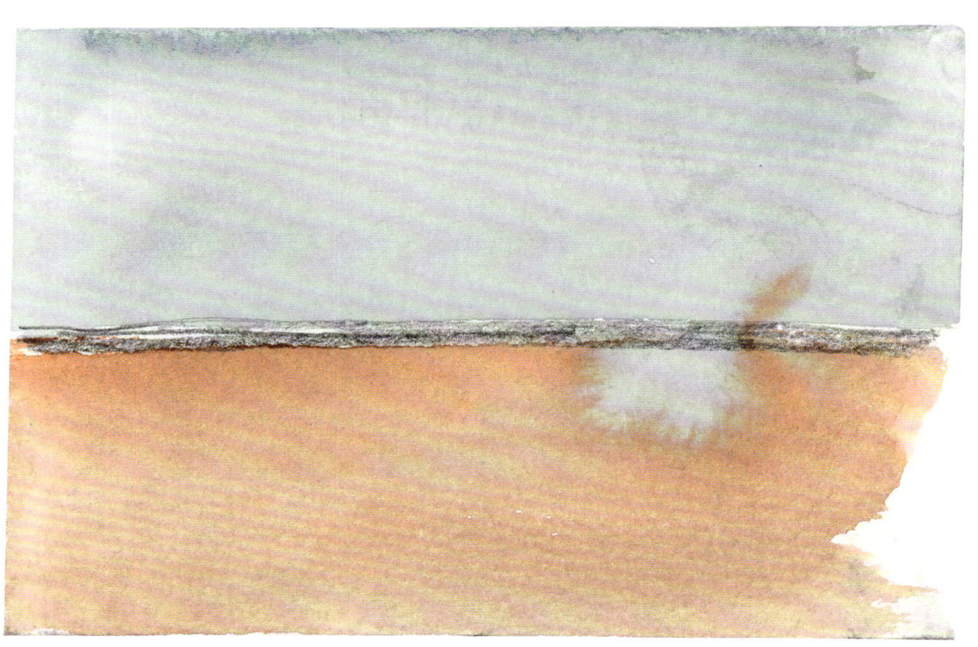

31. Piano Nobile 2017 oil on linen 70 x 90 in 177.8 x 228.6 cm

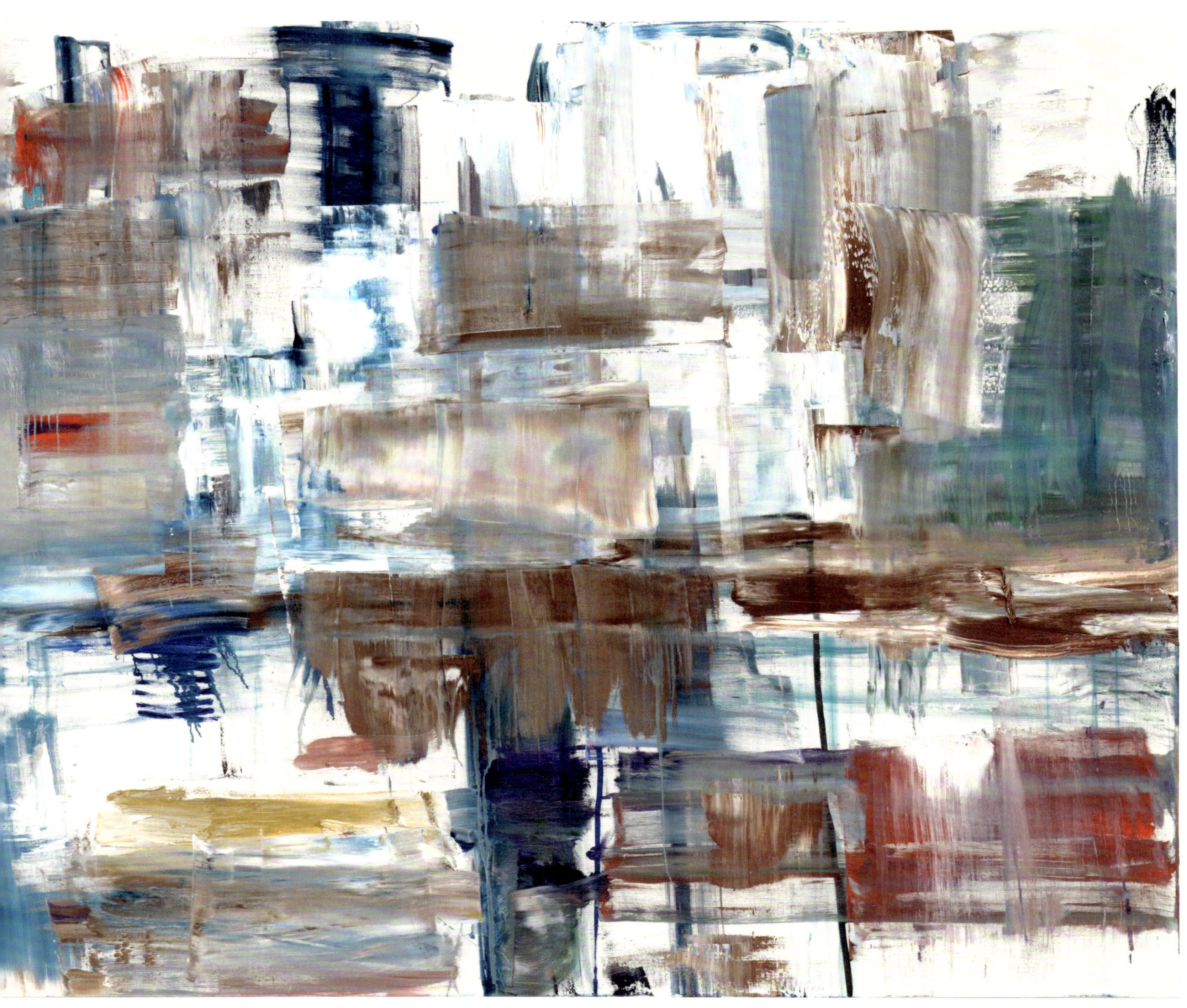

32. Untitled 2016 egg tempera on paper 7 x 10 1/4 in 17.8 x 26 cm

33. The Arrows of Emotion 2017 oil on linen 48 x 32 in 121.9 x 81.3 cm

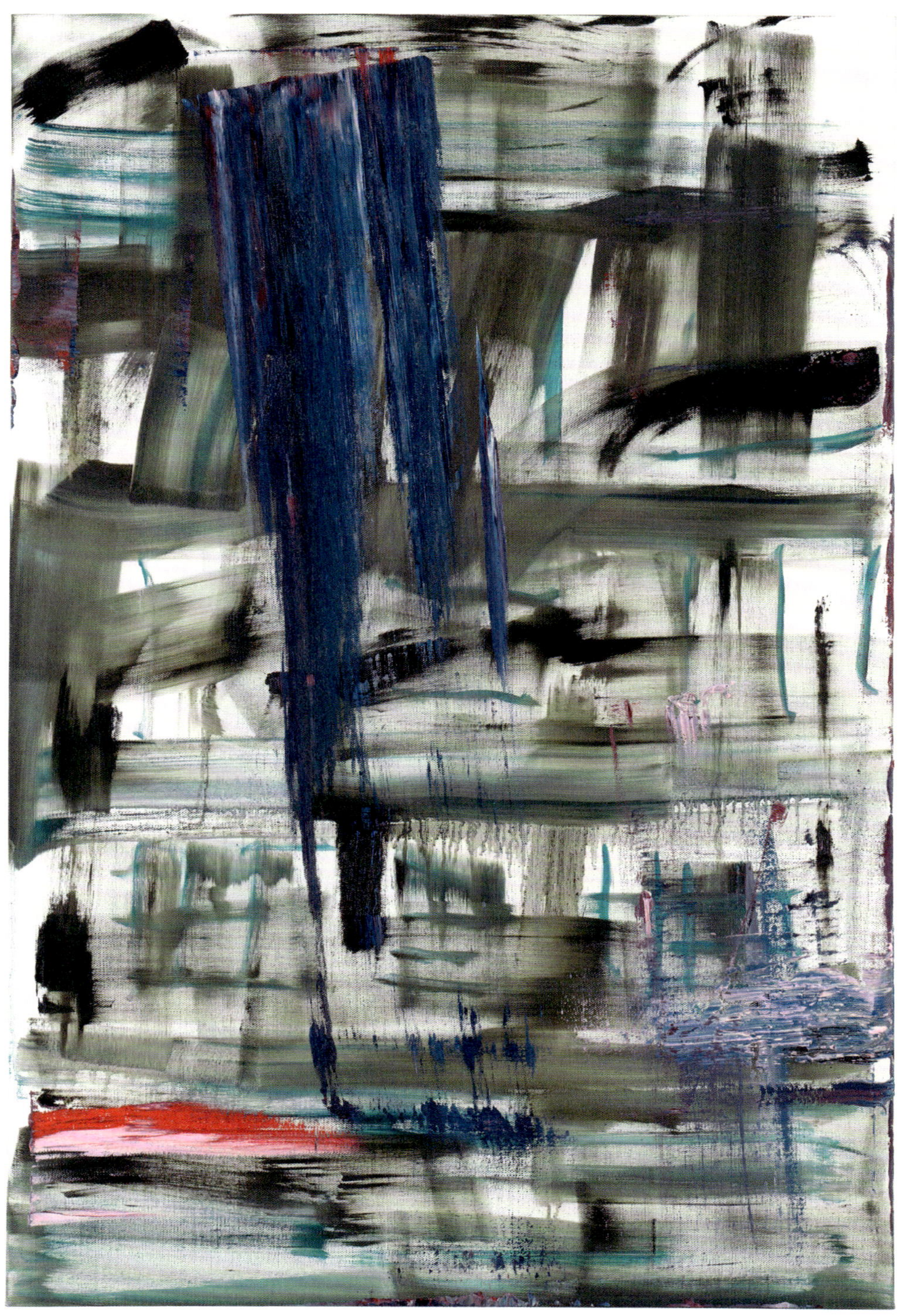

34. Untitled 2016 egg tempera on paper 5 3/4 x 8 1/4 in 14.6 x 21 cm

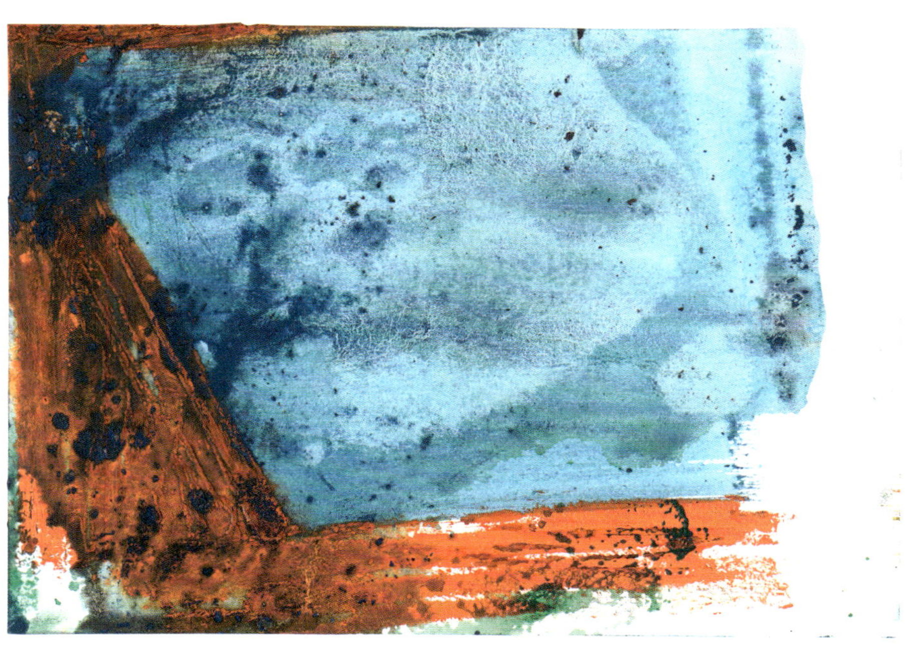

35. Coda Di Rospo 2017 oil on linen 70 x 88 in 177.8 x 223.5 cm

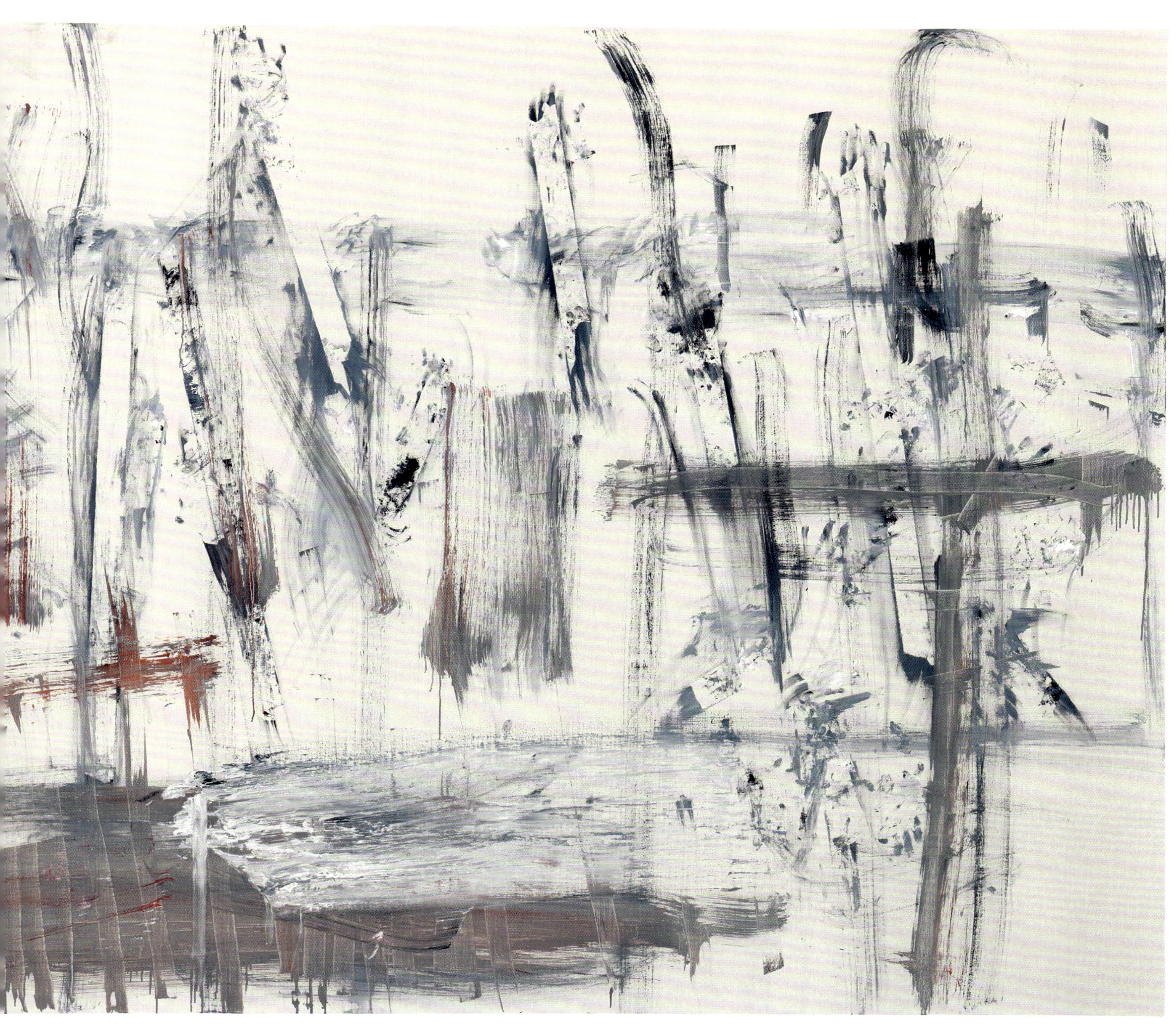

36. Untitled 2016 egg tempera on paper 8 1/4 x 8 1/4 in 21 x 21 cm

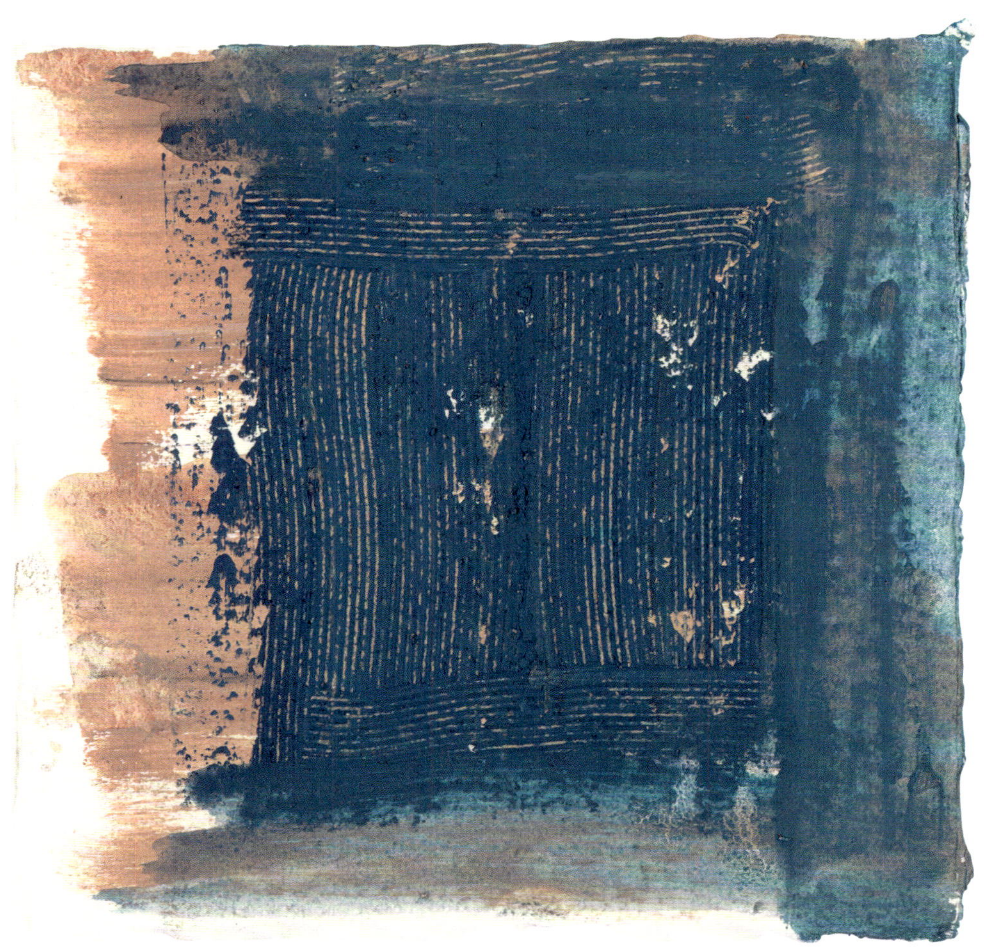

37. Apotheosis 2017 oil on linen 66 x 55 in 167.6 x 139.7 cm

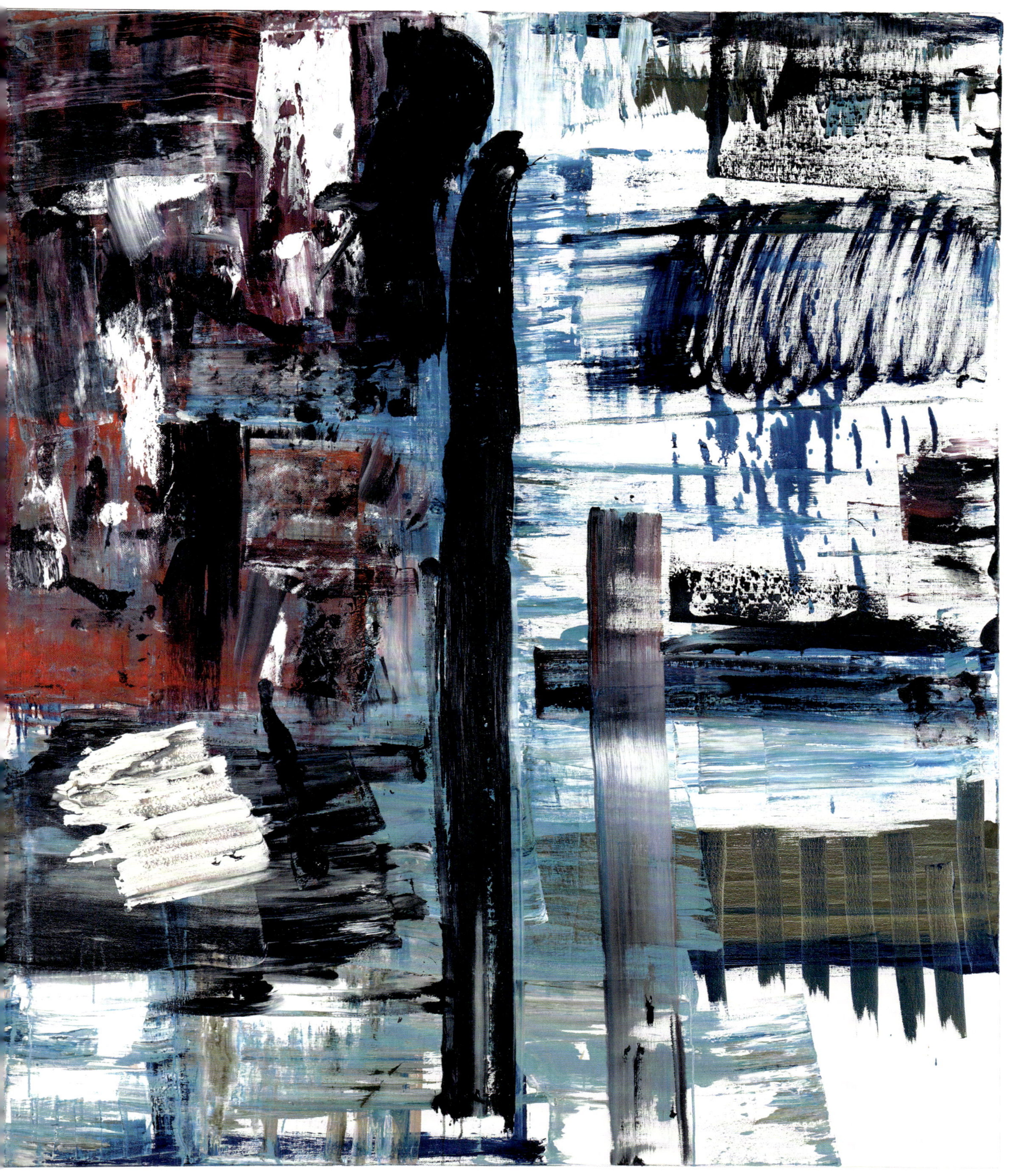

38. Untitled 2016 watercolor and colored pencil on paper 9 x 12 1/4 in 22.9 x 31.1 cm

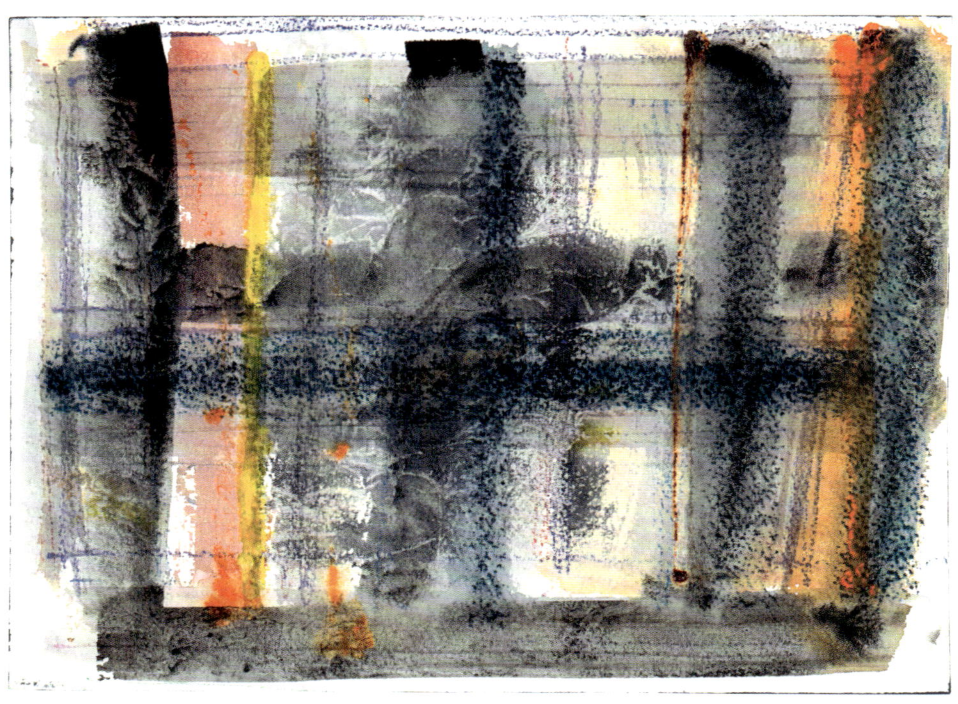

39. Antica Locanda Montin 2016 oil on linen 60 x 50 in 152.4 x 127 cm

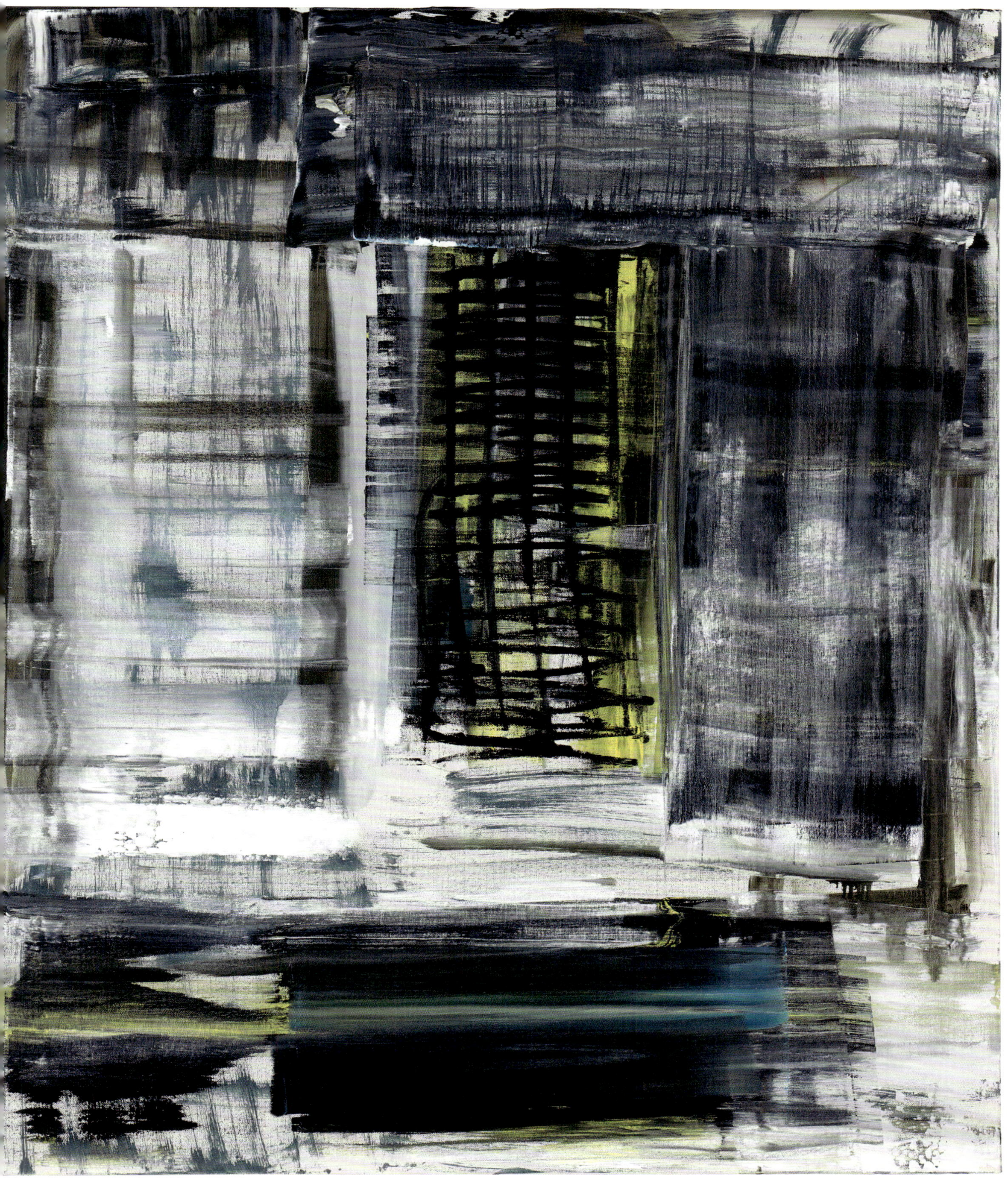

40. Untitled 2016 egg tempera and ink on paper 10 1/4 x 7 in 26 x 17.8 cm

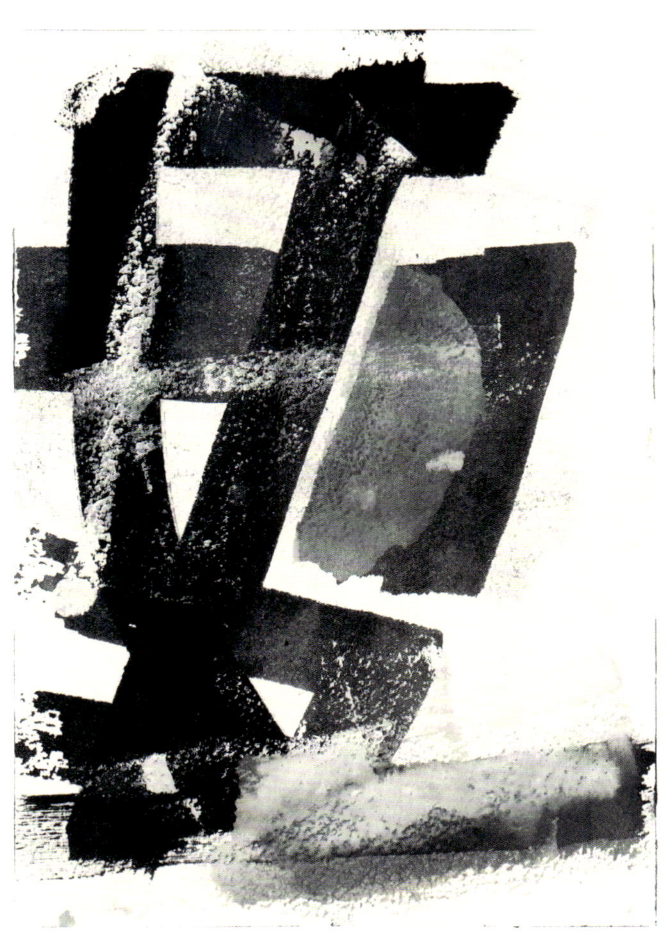

41. Mon Semblable Mon Frère 2017 oil on linen 50 x 30 in 127 x 76.2 cm

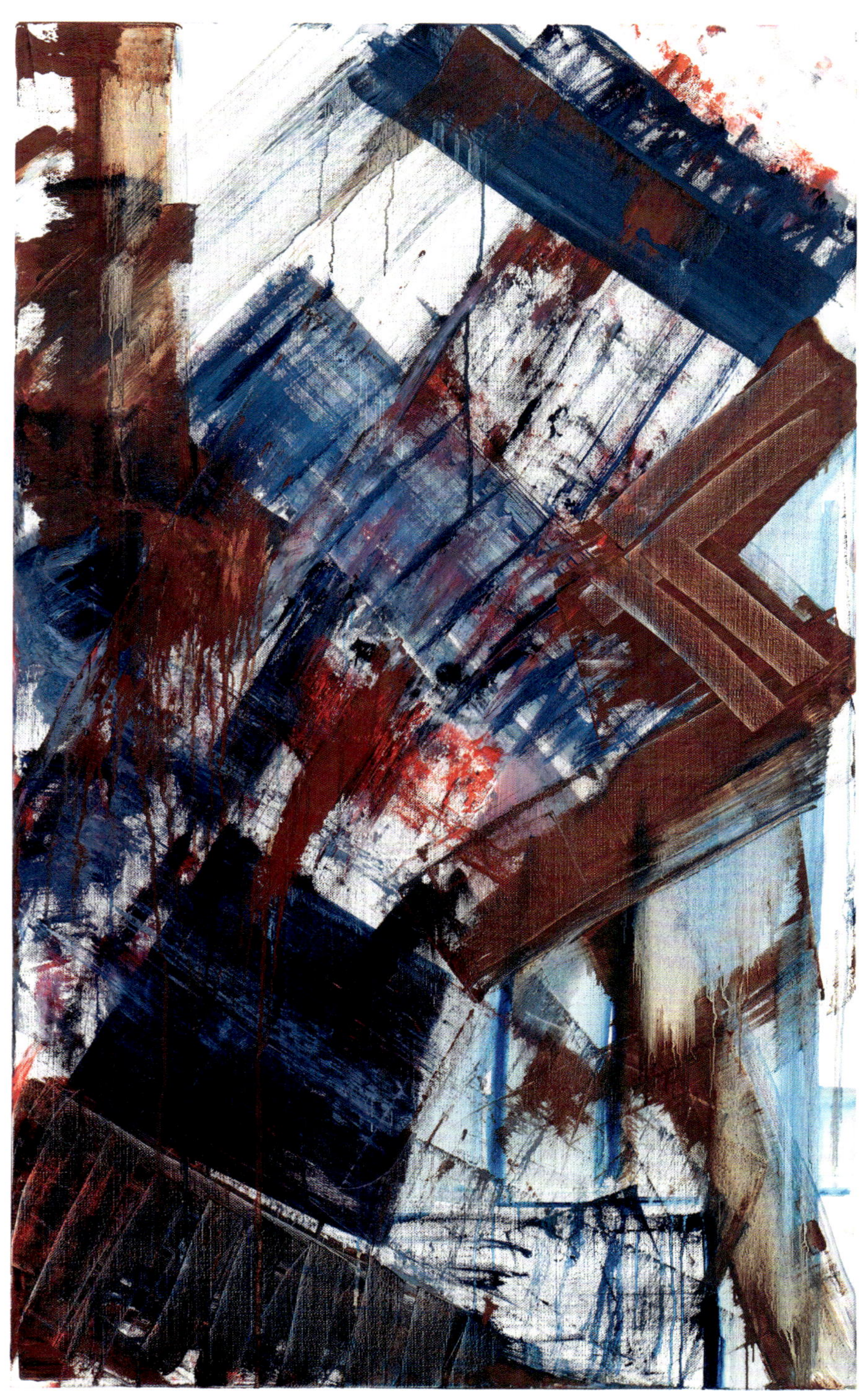

42. Untitled 2016 egg tempera on paper 4 x 6 in 10.2 x 15.2 cm

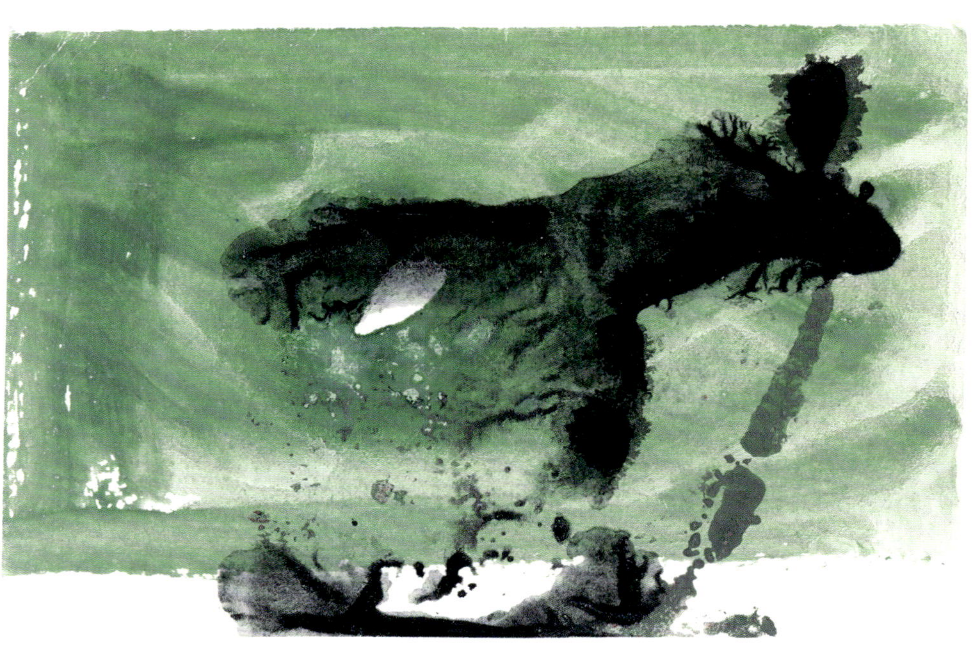

43. Versicle 2017 oil on linen 48 x 32 in 121.9 x 81.3 cm

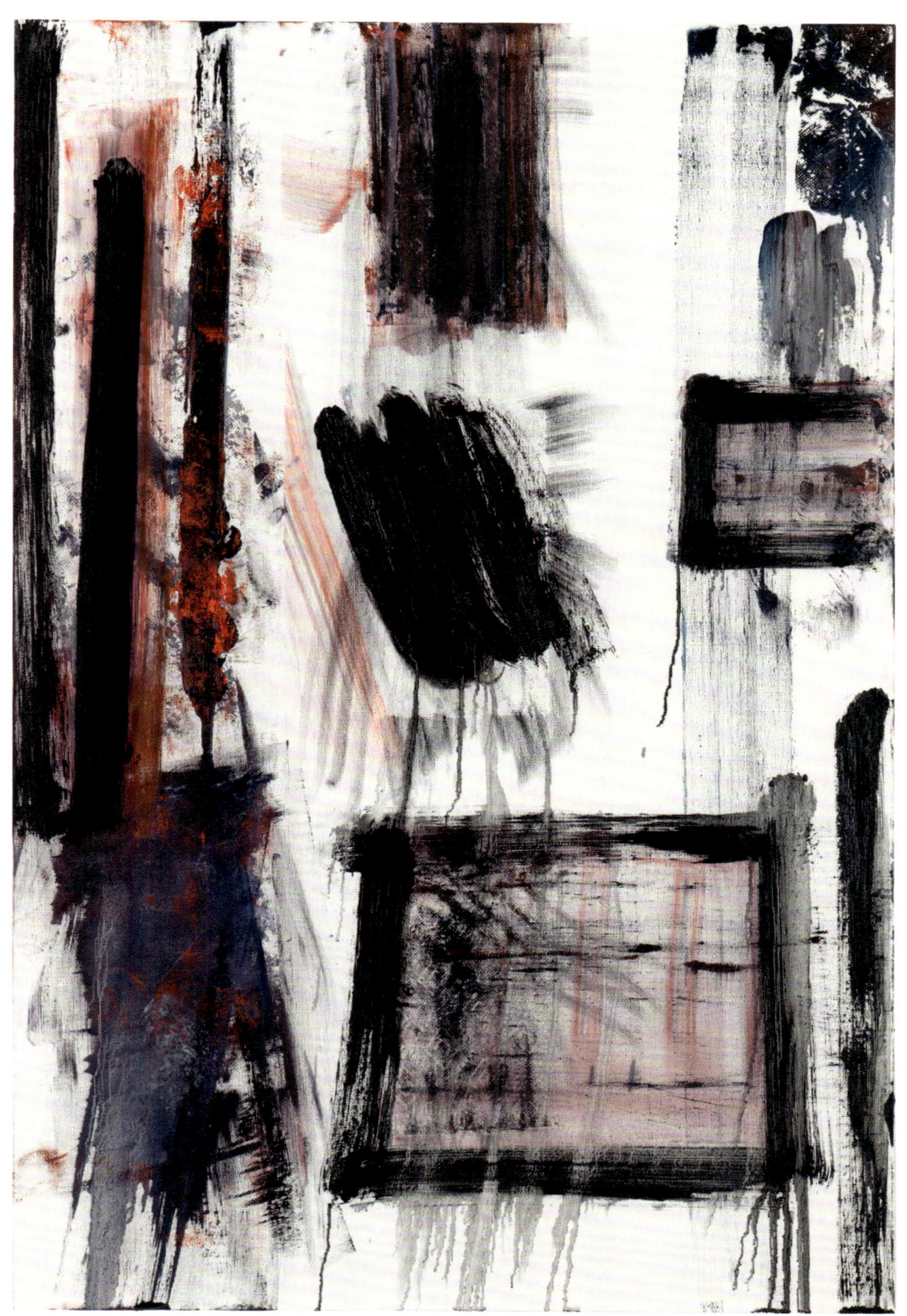

44. Sharps and Flats 2017 oil on linen 70 x 90 in 177.8 x 228.6 cm

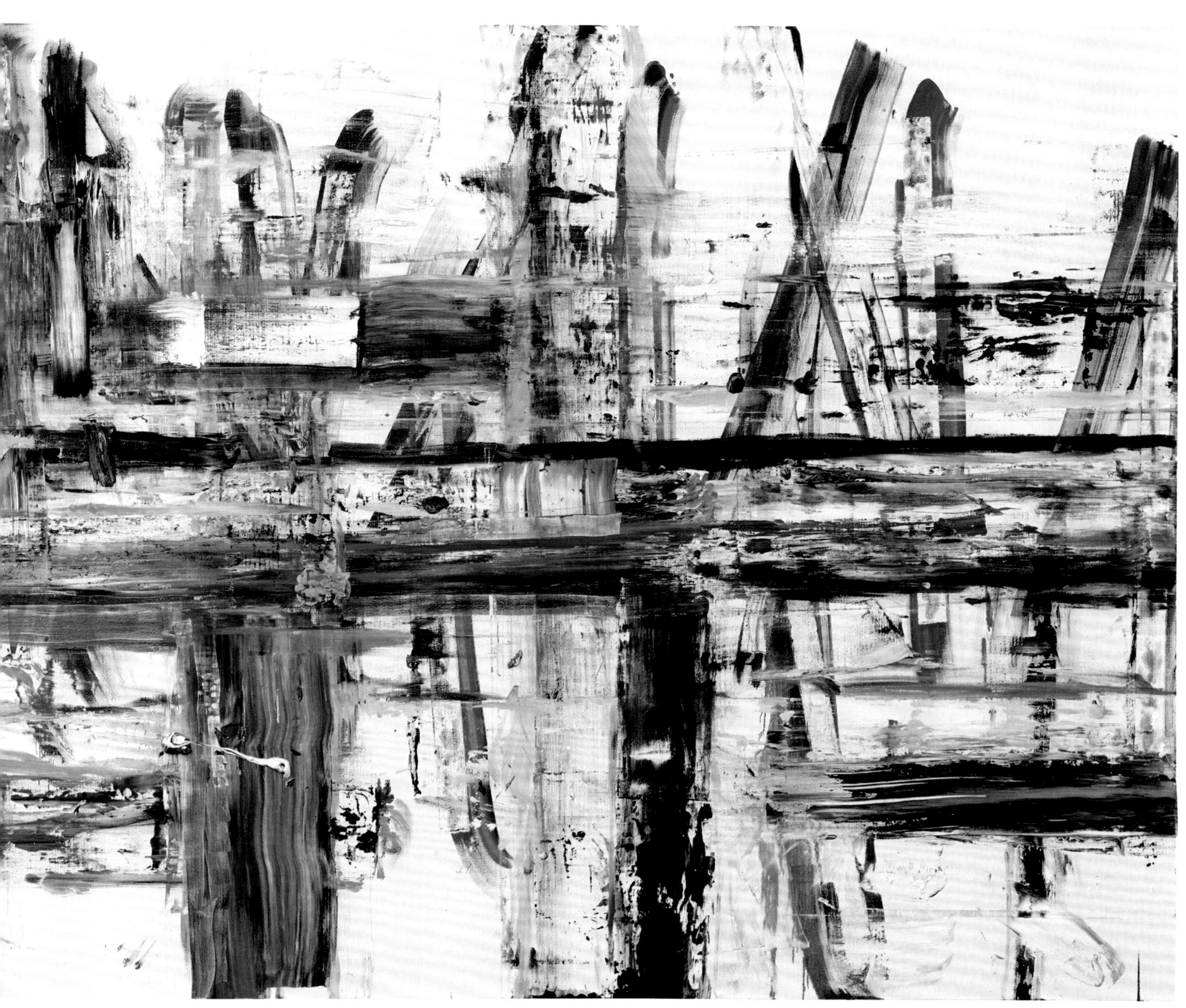

45. Untitled 2016 egg tempera, ink, and graphite on paper 5 3/4 x 8 1/4 in 14.6 x 21 cm

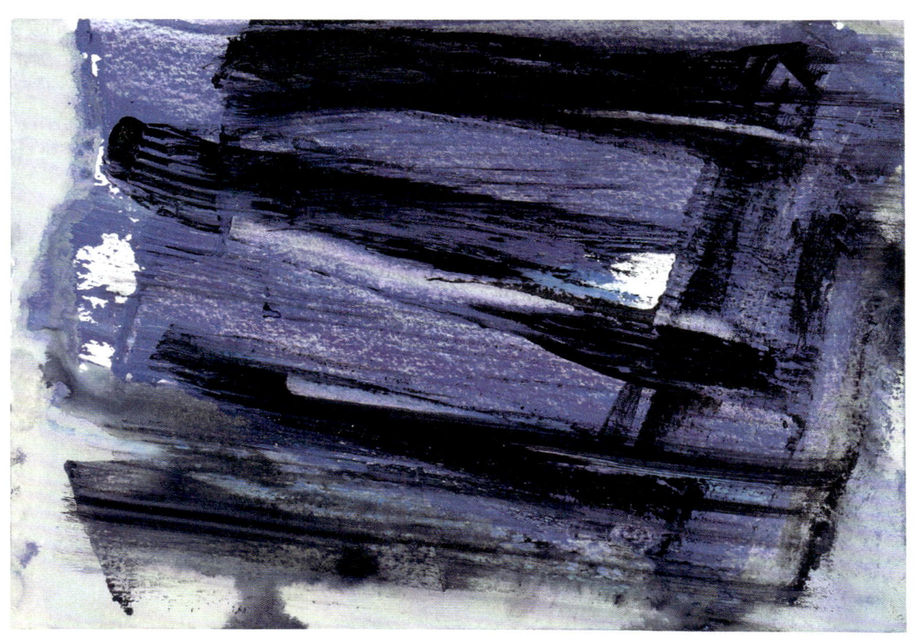

46. Cadence 2017 oil on linen 66 x 55 in 167.6 x 139.7 cm

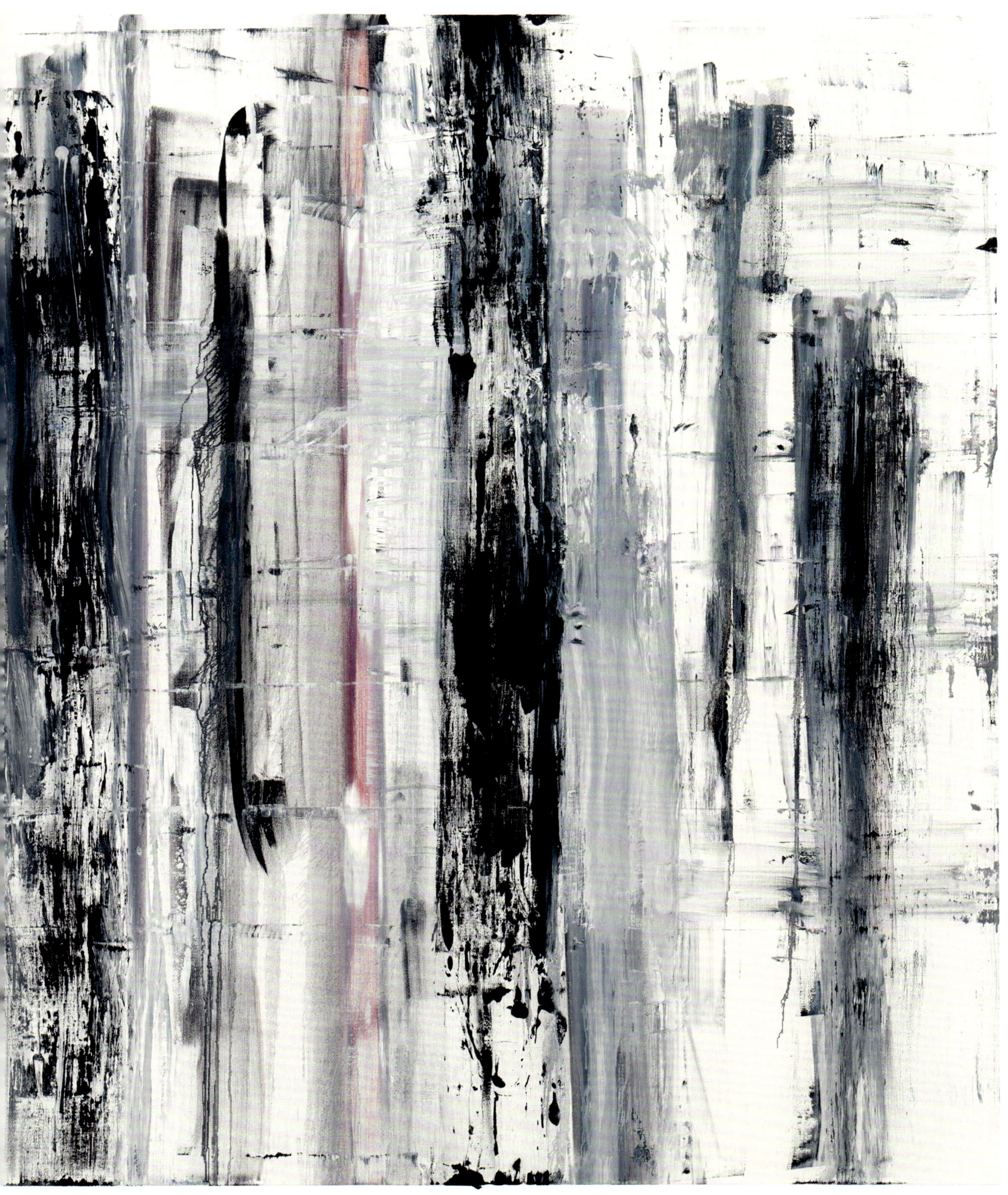

47. San Stae 2017 oil on linen 72 x 96 in 182.9 x 243.8 cm

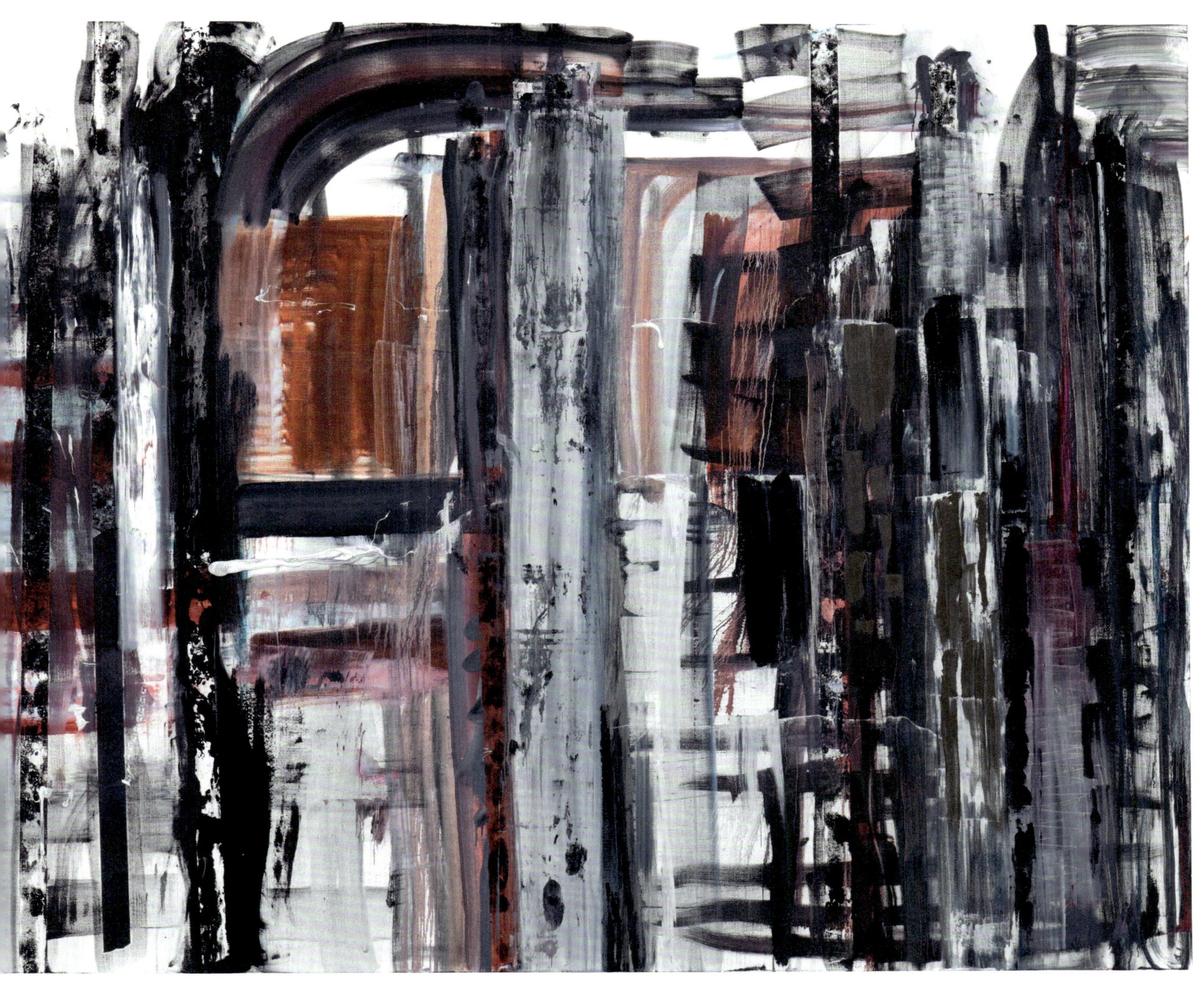

48. Monongahela 2017 oil on linen 66 x 55 in 167.6 x 139.7 cm

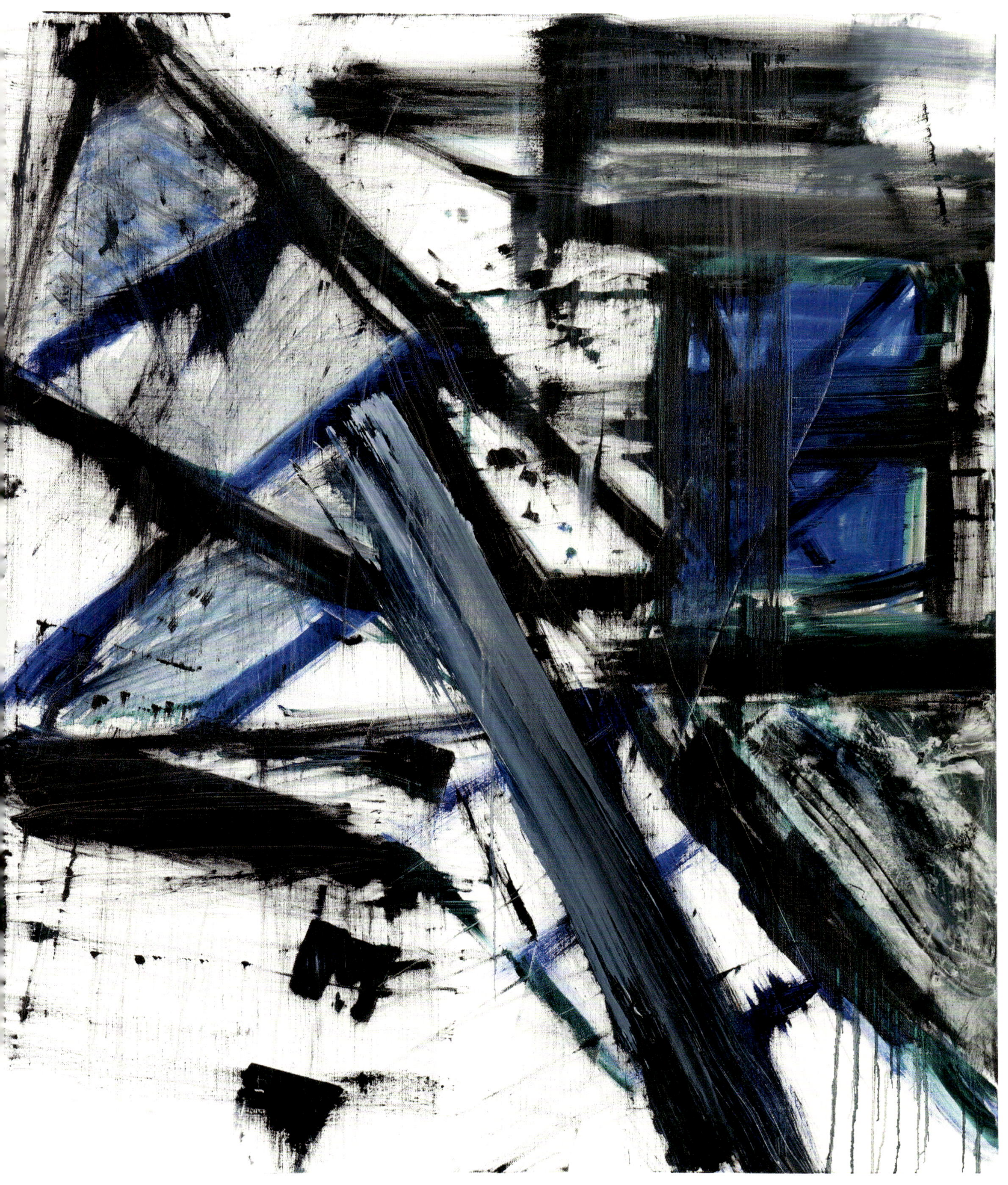

BIOGRAPHY

1939 Born in Philadelphia
1965 Moves to New York City

Lives and works in New York City and Decatur, New York

EDUCATION

1956–57 Philadelphia College of Art, Philadelphia
1958 Pennsylvania Academy of Fine Arts, Philadelphia
1963 B.F.A. and B.S., Tyler School of Fine Arts, Elkins Park, Pennsylvania
1965 M.F.A., University of Illinois at Urbana-Champaign

SOLO EXHIBITIONS

2017 *Louise Fishman*, Cheim & Read, New York

2016 *Louise Fishman: A Retrospective*, curated by Helaine Posner, Neuberger Museum, State University of New York at Purchase; traveled to Weatherspoon Art Museum, University of North Carolina at Greensboro
Paper Louise Tiny Fishman Rock, curated by Ingrid Schaffner, Institute of Contemporary Art, University of Pennsylvania, Philadelphia

2015 *Louise Fishman*, Cheim & Read, New York

2014 *Louise Fishman – Venice Watercolours 2011–2013*, Gallery Nosco, London

2013 *Louise Fishman: It's Here – Elsewhere*, Goya Contemporary, Baltimore, Maryland

2012 *Louise Fishman*, Cheim & Read, New York
Louise Fishman: Paintings, Drawings & Prints, John Davis Gallery, Hudson, New York
Louise Fishman: Five Decades, curated by Simon Watson, Jack Tilton Gallery, New York

2010 *Louise Fishman*, Gallery Paule Anglim, San Francisco

2009 *Louise Fishman: Among the Old Masters*, John & Mable Ringling Museum of Art, Sarasota, Florida
Louise Fishman, Cheim & Read, New York

2008 *Louise Fishman: Between Geometry and Gesture*, Galerie Kienzle & Gmeiner, Berlin

2007 *Louise Fishman, The Tenacity of Painting: Paintings from 1970 to 2005*, Hood Museum of Art, Dartmouth College, Hanover, New Hampshire

2006 *Louise Fishman*, Cheim & Read, New York

2005 *Louise Fishman*, Foster-Gwin, San Francisco

2004 *Louise Fishman, Recent Work*, Manny Silverman Gallery, Los Angeles
New York Abstract Painters George McNeil / Louise Fishman, Foster-Gwin, San Francisco

2003 *Louise Fishman*, Cheim & Read, New York

2002 *Louise Fishman*, Manny Silverman Gallery, Los Angeles

2001 *Louise Fishman*, Paule Anglim Gallery, San Francisco

2000 *Louise Fishman*, Cheim & Read, New York

1999 *Louise Fishman*, Paule Anglim Gallery, San Francisco

1998 *Louise Fishman: Paintings & Drawings*, Rhona Hoffman Gallery, Chicago
Louise Fishman: Recent Paintings and Drawings, Cheim & Read, New York

1996 *Louise Fishman: Recent Paintings*, Robert Miller Gallery, New York

1995 *Small Paintings*, Robert Miller Gallery, New York

1994 *Small Paintings, 1992–1994*, Bianca Lanza Gallery, Miami

1993 *Louise Fishman*, Robert Miller Gallery, New York

1992 *Louise Fishman: Small Paintings, 1979–1992*, Temple Gallery, Tyler School of Art, Philadelphia
Drawings and Experimental Work, 1971–1992, Tyler Gallery, Tyler School of Art, Philadelphia
Louise Fishman: Paintings, 1986–1992, Morris Gallery, Pennsylvania Academy of Fine Arts, Philadelphia
Louise Fishman: Small Paintings, 1978–1992, Simon Watson, New York, preview of exhibition held at Temple Gallery, Tyler School of Art, Philadelphia
Louise Fishman: Small Paintings, Olin Art Gallery, Kenyon College, Gambier, Ohio

1991 *Louise Fishman: New Paintings*, Lennon, Weinberg, Inc., New York

1989 *Louise Fishman: New Paintings 1987–1989*, Lennon, Weinberg, Inc., New York
Remembrance and Renewal, Simon Watson Gallery, New York

1987 *Louise Fishman and Andy Spence: Two from the Corcoran*, Winston Gallery, Washington, D.C.

1986 *Louise Fishman: New Paintings*, Baskerville & Watson Gallery, New York

1985 *Fishman/Sanderson*, North Carolina Museum of Art, Raleigh, North Carolina

1984 *Louise Fishman*, Baskerville & Watson Gallery, New York

1982 *Louise Fishman: Recent Work*, Oscarsson-Hood Gallery, New York
Louise Fishman, John Davis Gallery, Akron, Ohio

1980 *Louise Fishman: Small Paintings, The MacDowell Colony*, Oscarsson-Hood Gallery, New York

1979 *Louise Fishman*, Nancy Hoffman Gallery, New York
Louise Fishman: Five Years, 55 Mercer, New York

1978 *Louise Fishman*, Diplomat's Lobby, United States Department of State, Washington, D.C.

1977 *Louise Fishman*, Nancy Hoffman Gallery, New York

1976 *Louise Fishman*, University of Rhode Island, Kingston
Louise Fishman, John Doyle Gallery, Chicago

1974 *Louise Fishman*, Nancy Hoffman Gallery, New York

1964 *Louise Fishman*, Philadelphia Art Alliance, Philadelphia

GROUP EXHIBITIONS

2017 *Citings/Sightings*, Lennon, Weinberg, Inc., New York
Blue Black, curated by Glenn Ligon, Pulitzer Arts Foundation, St. Louis, Missouri
Art in Balance: Motorcycles and Fine Art, Susquehanna Art Museum, Harrisburg, Pennsylvania

2016 *#Pussypower*, curated by Jennifer Samet and Michael David, David & Schweitzer Contemporary, Brooklyn, New York
Leporelli Veneziani, curated by Berty Skuber, Emily Harvey Foundation, EHF Gallery, Venice
Your Face in the Mirror Isn't Your Face, Similar to Plastic Silverware, curated by Torey Thornton, Moran Bondaroff, Los Angeles
Golem, Jewish Museum, Berlin
Nice Weather, curated by David Salle, Skarstedt Gallery, New York
#makeamericagreatagain, curated by Raul Zamudio and Juan Puntes, co-curated by Blanca de la Torre, WhiteBox, New York

2015 *Intimacy in Discourse: Reasonable and Unreasonable Sized Paintings*, curated by Phong Bui, School of Visual Arts, New York
Painting 2.0: Expression in the Information Age, Museum Brandhorst, Germany; traveled to the Museum Moderner Kunst Stiftung Ludwig Wien (MUMOK), Vienna
A Few Days, Lennon, Weinberg, Inc., New York
Art AIDS America, Tacoma Art Museum, Tacoma, Washington; traveled to Zuckerman Museum of Art, Kennesaw State University, Kennesaw, Georgia; Bronx Museum of the Arts, New York; Alphawood Foundation, Chicago
Perfect Present: Three Generations of Painting, Louise Fishman, Rosanna Bruno, Odessa Straub, Jeffrey Stark, New York

2014 *De-Pict*, Gallery Nosco, London
Making Art Dance: Artists Donate Work to Benefit the Armitage Gone!, Mana

Contemporary, Jersey City, New Jersey
Whitney Museum of American Art 2014 Biennial Exhibition, Whitney Museum of American Art, New York
In Residence: Contemporary Artists at Dartmouth, Hood Museum of Art, Dartmouth College, Hanover, New Hampshire

2013 *Reinventing Abstraction: New York Painting in the 1980s*, curated by Raphael Rubinstein, Cheim & Read, New York

2012 *PAPYRI: Guestbooks, Bookworks and Similar Departures by Guests of Harvey Foundation 2004–2012*, Emily Harvey Foundation, Venice
Generations: Louise Fishman, Gertrude Fisher-Fishman, and Razel Kapustin, Woodmere Art Museum, Philadelphia

2011 *Dance/Draw*, Institute of Contemporary Art, Boston; traveled to Grey Art Gallery, New York University, New York; Frances Young Tang Teaching Museum and Art Gallery, Skidmore College, Saratoga Springs, New York
Abstraction, Albert Merola Gallery, Provincetown, Massachusetts
The Women in Our Life: A Fifteen-Year Anniversary Exhibition, Cheim & Read, New York
Seeing Gertrude Stein: Five Stories, Contemporary Jewish Museum, San Francisco; traveled to National Portrait Gallery, Washington, D.C.
To the Venetians, Rhode Island School of Design, Providence, Rhode Island
READYKEULOUS/The Hurtful Healer: The Correspondance Issue, Invisible-Exports, New York

2010 *Painting & Sculpture: To Benefit the Foundation for Contemporary Arts*, Lehmann Maupin Gallery, New York
LES FEMMES, McClain Gallery, Houston, Texas
Abstraction Revisited, Chelsea Art Museum, New York
Shifting the Gaze: Painting and Feminism, Jewish Museum, New York
Le Tableau: French Abstraction and its Affinities, curated by Joe Fyfe, Cheim & Read, New York

2009 *Les Femmes*, McClain Gallery, Houston, Texas
Before Again: Joan Mitchell, Louise Fishman, Harriet Korman, Melissa Meyer, Jill Moser, Denyse Thomasos, Lennon, Weinberg, Inc., New York
The Ringling International Arts Festival, John and Mable Ringling Museum of Art, Sarasota, Florida
Abstractions by Gallery Artists, Cheim & Read, New York
Propose: Works on Paper from the 1970s, Alexander Gray Associates, New York

2008 *MassArt at the Fine Arts Work Center: Faculty and Visiting Artists*, Hudson D. Walker Gallery Fine Arts Work Center, Provincetown, Massachusetts
Pretty Ugly, curated by Alison Gingeras, Maccarone Gallery and Gavin Brown's Enterprise, New York
Significant Form: The Persistence of Abstraction, Pushkin State Museum of Fine Arts, Moscow
Environments and Empires, Rose Art Museum, Brandeis University, Waltham, Massachusetts

2007 *American Abstract*, Maruani & Noirhomme Gallery, Knokke, Belgium
Short Distance to Now Part #2: Paintings from New York 1967–1975, Galerie Thomas Flor, Düsseldorf, Germany
The Fluid Fields: Abstraction and Reference, Tyler Galleries, Tyler School of Art, Philadelphia
WACK! Art and the Feminist Revolution, Geffen Contemporary at the Museum of Contemporary Art, Los Angeles; traveled to National Museum of Women in the Arts, Washington, D.C.; MoMA P.S. 1, Long Island City, New York; Vancouver Art Gallery, Vancouver

2006 *High Times, Hard Times: New York Painting 1965–75*, curated by Katy Siegal, Independent Curators International, Weatherspoon Art Museum, University of North Carolina at Greensboro; traveled to American University Museum at the Katzen Arts Center, Washington, D.C.; National Academy Museum, New York; Museo Tamayo Arte Contemporáneo,

Mexico City, Mexico; Neue Galerie Graz, Graz, Austria; ZKM | Center for Art and Media Karlsruhe, Karlsruhe, Germany
The New Landscape / The New Still Life: Soutine and Modern Art, Cheim & Read, New York
The Name of this Show Is Not Gay Art Now, Paul Kasmin Gallery, New York

2005 *Looking at Words: The Formal Presence of Text in Modern and Contemporary Works on Paper*, Andrea Rosen Gallery, New York
PAINT, Elizabeth Leach Gallery, Portland, Oregon
Contemporary Women Artists: New York, University Art Gallery, Indiana State University, Terre Haute, Indiana

2004 *Summer Invitational*, Nielsen Gallery, Boston
Twelve from Cheim & Read, Fay Gold Gallery, Atlanta, Georgia
Drawing Exhibition, Galerie S 65 Cologne, Germany

2003 *The Invisible Thread: Buddhist Spirit in Contemporary Art*, Newhouse Center for Contemporary Art, Snug Harbor Cultural Center, Staten Island, New York
Women's Lines, G Fine Art, Washington, D.C.
Grisaille, James Graham & Sons, New York

2002 *Zenroxy*, Von Lintel Gallery, New York
Nocturne / Nocturnal, Skoto Gallery, New York
Personal and Political: The Woman's Art Movement, 1969–1975, Guild Hall Museum, East Hampton, New York
Art Downtown: New York Painting and Sculpture, Wall Street Rising, 48 Wall Street, New York
177th Annual Exhibition, National Academy of Design, New York
Painting: A Passionate Response, Sixteen American Artists, The Painting Center, New York
Nature Found and Made, Chambers Fine Art, New York

2001 *Four Painters*, Lindsey Brown, New York
Watercolor: In the Abstract, curated by Pamela Auchincloss, The Hyde Collection, Glens Falls, New York; traveled to Michael C. Rockefeller Arts Center Gallery, State University of New York at Fredonia; Butler Institute of American Art, Youngstown, Ohio; Nina Freundenheim, Inc., Buffalo, New York; Ben Shahn Gallery for Visual Arts, William Patterson University, Wayne, New Jersey; Sarah Moody Gallery of Art, University of Alabama at Tuscaloosa
Seven Female Visionaries Before Feminism, Mills College Art Museum, Oakland, California
Opening Exhibition, Lesbian and Gay Community Services Center, New York
Imaging Judaism/Mining History, Susquehanna Art Museum, Harrisburg, Pennsylvania
Invitational Exhibition of Painting and Sculpture, American Academy of Arts and Letters, New York

2000 *Snapshot: An Exhibition of 1000 Artists*, The Contemporary, Baltimore, Maryland
The Perpetual Well: Contemporary Art from the Collection of the Jewish Museum, Parrish Art Museum, Southampton, New York
Painting Abstraction, New York Studio School, New York
175th Annual Exhibition, National Academy of Design, New York

1999 *Drawing in the Present Tense*, Parsons School of Design, New York
Walking, Danese, New York
American Abstraction / American Realism: The Great Debate, curated by Jonathan Van Dyke, Susquehanna Art Museum, Harrisburg, Pennsylvania
Severed Ear: The Poetry of Abstraction, Creiger-Dane Gallery, Boston
Gestural Abstraction, Times Square Gallery, Hunter College, New York

1998 *Paintings & Drawings*, Rhona Hoffman Gallery, Chicago
San Francisco International Art Exposition, Cheim & Read Exhibition Booth, San Francisco

Undercurrents & Overtones: Contemporary Abstract Painting, California College of the Arts, Wattis Institute for Contemporary Arts, Oakland, California
Small Paintings, Cheim & Read, New York

1997 *Convergence*, George Billis Gallery, New York
Voices: The Power of Abstraction, Eighth Floor Gallery, New York
Abstract Painting, curated by Jeffrey Wasserman, Carrie Haddad Gallery, Hudson, New York
Basically Black & White, Neuberger Museum, State University of New York at Purchase
Retreat and Renewal: The Painters and Sculptors of the MacDowell Colony, Currier Gallery of Art, Manchester, New Hampshire; traveled to Equitable Gallery, New York; Wichita Art Museum, Wichita, Kansas; Fort Wayne Museum of Art, Fort Wayne, Indiana
Affinities with the East, Robert Miller Gallery, New York
After the Fall: Aspects of Abstract Painting since 1970, Newhouse Center for Contemporary Art, Snug Harbor Cultural Center, Staten Island

1996 *Women's Work*, Greene Naftali, New York
Transforming the Social Order, Tyler Galleries, Tyler School of Art, Temple University, Philadelphia
Summer Group Show, Robert Miller Gallery, New York

1995 *New Faculty*, Harvard University, Carpenter Center for the Visual Arts, Cambridge, Massachusetts
25 Americans: Painting the '90s, Milwaukee Art Museum, Wisconsin
Artist's Choice: Elizabeth Murray, Museum of Modern Art, New York
1995 Carnegie International, Carnegie Museum of Art, Pittsburgh, Pennsylvania

1994 *Small and Wet: Abstract Painting and Sculpture*, Bernard Toale Gallery, Boston
46th Annual Academy Purchase Exhibition, American Academy of Arts and Letters, New York

Consecrations: The Spiritual in Art in the Time of AIDS, Museum of Contemporary Religious Art, Saint Louis University, St. Louis, Missouri
Couples, Elga Wimmer, New York
Relatively Speaking: Mothers and Daughters in Art, Sweet Briar College, Sweet Briar, Virginia; traveled to Newhouse Center for Contemporary Art, Snug Harbor Cultural Center, Staten Island, New York; Rahr West Museum, Manitowoc, Wisconsin
Abstract Works on Paper, Robert Miller Gallery, New York

1993 *30th Anniversary Exhibition of Drawings, to benefit the Foundation for Contemporary Performance Arts, Inc.*, Castelli Gallery, New York
Singularities, Blondies Contemporary Art, New York
The Linear Image II, Marisa del Re Gallery, New York
The Inaugural Show, The Painting Center, New York
Art Discovery '93, Cooperstown Art Association and Smithy-Pioneer Gallery, Cooperstown, New York
Soho Abstract-Figurative, Robert Miller Gallery, New York
Drawing the Line Against AIDS, under the aegis of the 45th Venice Biennale, Peggy Guggenheim Collection, Venice; reinstalled at the Guggenheim Museum, Soho, New York

1992 *Paintings by Martha Diamond, Mary Heilmann, Harriet Korman, Louise Fishman and Bernard Piffaretti*, Robert Miller Gallery, New York
The Jewish Museum's Masked Ball in Celebration of Purim, Jewish Museum, New York

1991 *Act-Up Benefit*, Matthew Marks Gallery, New York
Spring/Summer Exhibition, Part One: Painters, Lennon, Weinberg, Inc., New York
Something Pithier and More Psychological, Simon Watson Gallery, New York
Twentieth-Century Collage, Margo Leavin Gallery, Los Angeles; traveled to Centro Cultural Arte Contemporaneo, Polonco, Mexico; Musèe d'Art Moderne et d'Art Contemporain (MAMAC), Nice, France

1990 *From Earth to Archetype*, LedisFlam Gallery, New York
Group Exhibition of Gallery Artists, Lennon, Weinberg, Inc., New York
A Group Exhibition, Lennon, Weinberg, Inc., New York

1989 *Belief in Paint: Eleven Contemporary Artists*, Usdan Gallery, Bennington College, Bennington, Vermont
Fragments of History, Albany Museum of Art, Albany, Georgia
A Decade of American Drawing 1980–1989, Daniel Weinberg Gallery, Los Angeles
Works on Paper, Lennon, Weinberg, Inc., New York
Towards Form, Greenberg, Wilson Gallery, New York
A Group Exhibition, Lennon, Weinberg, Inc., New York

1988 *Golem: Danger, Deliverance and Art*, Jewish Museum, New York
Selections from the Edward R. Downe, Jr. Collection, curated by Klaus Kertess, Davis-McClain Gallery, Houston, Texas
Louise Fishman, David Reed, Joan Mitchell, curated by Marjorie Welish, Barbara Toll Gallery, New York

1987 The Parrish Art Museum, Southampton, New York
40th Biennial Exhibition of Contemporary American Painting, Corcoran Gallery of Art, Washington, D.C.
Whitney Museum of American Art 1987 Biennial Exhibition, Whitney Museum of American Art, New York

1986 *Artists for Pride*, Nexus Gallery, Philadelphia
Louise Fishman, Hermine Ford and Arthur Cohen, Hofstra University, New York
Jewish Themes / Contemporary American Artists II, Jewish Museum, New York; traveled to Spertus Museum of Judaica, Chicago; National Museum of Jewish History, Philadelphia
Heland Thorden Wetterling Galleries, Stockholm
Spirit Tracks – Big Abstract Drawings, Pratt Manhattan Center Gallery, New York and Pratt Institute Gallery, Brooklyn, New York
Baskerville & Watson Gallery, New York

1985 *Drawings 1975–1985*, Barbara Toll Fine Arts, New York
Baskerville & Watson Gallery, New York
Painting as Landscape, curated by Klaus Kertess, Parrish Art Museum, Southampton, New York; traveled to Baxter Art Gallery, Pasadena, California
An Invitational, curated by Tiffany Bell, Condeso/Lawler, New York
Paintings 1985, Pam Adler Gallery, New York
Twelve Painters and Six Sculptors, Tyler Galleries, Tyler School of Art, Temple University, Philadelphia

1984 *Relief Prints Since 1980*, Summit Art Center, Summit, New Jersey
Second Nature: Abstract Drawings and Paintings, curated by John Lee and Tom Wolf, Proctor Art Center, Bard College, Annandale-on-Hudson, New York
Cable Gallery, New York
New Prints Since 1980, Phillip Johnson Center, Muhlenberg College, Allentown, Pennsylvania

1983 *Six Painters*, Hudson River Museum, Yonkers, New York
Drawing In and Out, Baskerville & Watson, New York
Painting from the Mind's Eye, Hillwood Art Gallery, Long Island University, Greenvale, New York

1982 Washburn Gallery, New York
Abstraction, Neuberger Museum, State University of New York at Purchase
Susanne Hilberry Gallery, Birmingham, Michigan
Mixing Art and Politics, Randolph Street Gallery, Chicago
Five New York Artists: Stuart Diamond, Louise Fishman, Guy Goodwin, Bill Jensen, Judy Pfaff, Suzanne Lemberg Usdan Gallery, Bennington College, Bennington, Vermont
Abstract Painting: Substance and Meaning – Painting by Woman Artists, New York Chapter of the Women's Caucus for Art, New York
Painterly Abstraction, Fort Wayne Museum, Fort Wayne, Indiana

1981 *CAPS Award Winners in Painting 1980–1981*, Proctor Art Center, Bard College and Munson Williams Proctor Museum, Utica, New York
CAPS Grantees from Brooklyn, Brooklyn Museum, New York
Rush Rhees Fine Arts Gallery, University of Rochester, New York
1981 Painting Invitational, Oscarsson-Hood Gallery, New York

1980 *Inaugural Exhibit*, Oscarsson-Hood Gallery, New York
Work on Paper, Mary Boone Gallery, New York

1979 *Major New Works*, Nancy Hoffman Gallery, New York

1977 *Critic's Choice*, Joe and Emily Lowe Art Gallery, Syracuse University, Syracuse, New York; traveled to Munson-Williams-Proctor Arts Institute Museum of Art, Utica, New York
Fifth Anniversary Show, Nancy Hoffman Gallery, New York
Paintings that Reveal the Wall, curated by Tom Wolf, Bard College, Annandale-on-Hudson, New York
Major New Works, Nancy Hoffman Gallery, New York
Nancy Hoffman in Oxford, Miami University, Oxford, Ohio
Preparatory Notes – Thinking Drawings, Part II, 80 Washington Square East Galleries, New York University, New York

1976 *Paris International Art Fair*, Grand Palais, Paris
Artist '76: A Celebration, Marion Koogler McNay Art Institute, San Antonio, Texas
University of Rhode Island, Kingston, Rhode Island

1975 John Doyle Gallery, Chicago
New York Faculty Exhibition, Proctor Art Center, Bard College, Annandale-on-Hudson, New York

1973 *A Woman's Group*, Nancy Hoffman Gallery, New York
Whitney Museum of American Art 1973 Biennial Exhibition, Whitney Museum of American Art, New York

1972 *Summer Show*, Paula Cooper Gallery, New York
Open A.I.R., A.I.R. Gallery, New York

1963 *National Watercolor and Drawing Exhibition*, Pennsylvania Academy of Fine Arts, Philadelphia

PUBLIC COLLECTIONS

American Academy of Arts and Letters, New York
Art Institute of Chicago
Baltimore Museum of Art, Maryland
Carnegie Museum of Art, Pittsburgh, Pennsylvania
Chrysler Museum of Art, Norfolk, Virginia
Denver Art Museum, Colorado
High Museum of Art, Atlanta, Georgia
Hood Museum of Art, Dartmouth College, Hanover, New Hampshire
Jewish Museum, New York
Kunstmuseum Liechtenstein, Vaduz, Liechtenstein
Metropolitan Museum of Art, New York
Museum of Contemporary Art, San Diego, California
National Museum of Women in the Arts, Washington, D.C.
Neuberger Museum, State University of New York at Purchase
University Museum of Contemporary Art, University of Massachusetts, Amherst
University of Michigan Museum of Art, Ann Arbor, Michigan
Woodmere Art Museum, Philadelphia

AWARDS

1963 Tyler School of Art, First Painting Prize, Student Exhibit
1974 Change, Inc., Artists Fellowship
1975 Tyler School of Art, Bertha Lowenburg Prize for the Senior Woman to Excel in Art
National Endowment for the Arts, Visual Artists Fellowship, Painting
1979 John Simon Guggenheim Memorial Foundation Fellowship in Fine Arts
1980 MacDowell Colony, Visual Artists Fellowship
1981 Creative Artists Public Service Program (CAPS) Fellowship in Painting
1983 National Endowment for the Arts, Visual Artists Fellowship, Painting
1986 New York Foundation for the Arts Fellowship in Painting
Adolph & Esther Gottlieb Foundation General Support Grant
1993 National Endowment for the Arts Visual Artists Fellowship, Painting
2002 Adolph & Clara Obrig Prize for Painting, National Academy of Design, 177th Annual Exhibition

Published on the occasion of the Cheim & Read exhibition, September 7–October 28, 2017.

Editorial Assistant Sarah Dansberger. Color separation Altaimage. Photography Brian Buckley. Printer Graphicom. ISBN 978-1-944316-08-2.

Louise Fishman

Cheim & Read
2017

Design John Cheim. Essay Aruna D'Souza. Editor Ellen Robinson.